EARTH
Our Original Monastery

"For so many people, the earth is sacred and creation is a sanctuary where we find the Divine Presence. But few have expressed the depth of this spiritual wisdom as insightfully as Christine Valters Paintner does in this book. *Earth, Our Original Monastery* is both a proclamation of the holiness of nature and a practical guide to meeting God in ordinary and humble ways."

Carl McColman
Author of *Befriending Silence*

"Practical and insightful, this beautiful book is perfect for any seeker of renewed contemplative styles and practices. It invites you to enter the creative side of your inner monastery and discover faith in fresh and relevant ways."

Br. Mickey McGrath, O.S.F.S.
Artist and storyteller

"*Earth, Our Original Monastery* is a love song—a sacred ecstatic chant in a language we somehow know. In her wise, gentle way, Christine Valters Paintner opens our eyes to the wonder under our feet, our ears to the poem Earth is speaking, and our hearts to answer 'Yes. Yes. This is my prayer, my cathedral, my home.'"

Janet Conner
Creator of the *Praying at the Speed of Love* podcast

"Convinced that creation pulses with the Divine Presence, Christine Valters Paintner leads us to fall in love with it. Taking her words to heart and following her suggestions for relishing nature will help you see the sacred in creation and call you to help alleviate the environmental crisis. *Earth, Our Original Monastery* is a unique and fascinating paean to God's sacred creatures."

Sr. Mary Kathleen Glavich, S.N.D.
Author of *Praying on Empty* and *Heart to Heart with Mary*

EARTH
Our Original Monastery

Cultivating Wonder

and Gratitude

through Intimacy

with Nature

Christine Valters Paintner

SORIN BOOKS   Notre Dame, IN

© 2020 by Christine Valters Paintner

www.sorinbooks.com

Paperback: ISBN-13 978-1-932057-20-1

E-book: ISBN-13 978-1-932057-21-8

Cover image © getty images.

Cover and text design by Brian C. Conley.

Printed and bound in the United States of America.

Library of Congress Cataloging-in-Publication Data is available.

To the canine companion teachers
I have had the privilege of knowing and loving:
Euri, Nicky, Duke, Tune, Winter, Ginger Nut,
Melba, Sisi, and Sourney

Let me seek, then, the gift of silence, and poverty, and solitude,
where everything I touch is turned into prayer:
where the sky is my prayer, the birds are my prayer,
the wind in the trees is my prayer, for God is in all.

–Thomas Merton, *Thoughts in Solitude*

Let no one think it ridiculous to learn a lesson in virtue from
    birds.
Does not Solomon instruct us:
    "Go to the ant thou sluggard, consider her ways and be
    wise"?
    –Bede, *The Age of Bede*

CONTENTS

INTRODUCTION

The monk here and now is supposed to be living the life
of the new creation in which the right relation to all the rest
of God's creatures is fully restored. Hence Desert Father stories
about tame lions and all that jazz.
—Thomas Merton, *Hidden Ground of Love: Letters*[1]

Of the many rich and fruitful paths available as part of the Christian tradition, the monastic way calls to me the strongest. The invitation to live life with more slowness, simplicity, and attentiveness is a rich gift in a world driven by speed, consumerism, and distraction. Contemplative practices help to offer an antidote to ways of living that have contributed to the destruction of Earth.

Monastic tradition has its roots in a call to be in intimate connection with nature. The monk's path was birthed in the forests and deserts, the places of wilderness and other wild edges that reflect an inner reality as well. This call to the edges, which is the monk's call, is a call to wildness—to that which lies beyond our domesticated, neat, safe, and secure lives. Nature reminds us of the messiness and beauty of things. Nature says that when we let ourselves get messy and play in the dirt, profound things can happen.

Our work as spiritual seekers and contemplatives is to see all of creation as woven together in holiness and to live this truth. In this loving act we begin to knit together that which has been torn; we gather all that has been scattered. Contemplative practice is a way to bring healing presence to the world.

The central image I offer in this book is to consider Earth as our original monastery. Earth is the place where we learn our most fundamental prayers, hear the call of the wild arising at dawn that awakens us to a new day, participate in the primal liturgy of praise unfolding all around us, and experience the wisdom and guidance of the seasons.

When I long to go on retreat, it is most often the sea or the forest that calls to me. When I lead others on retreat and ask participants where they most often experience a sense of sanctuary and renewal, the majority of responses are places in nature.

Everything in creation becomes a catalyst for my deepened self-understanding. The forest asks me to embrace my truth once again. The hummingbird invites me to sip holy nectar, the egret to stretch out my wings, the sparrows to remember my flock. Each pine cone contains an epiphany; each smooth stone offers a revelation. I watch and witness as the sun slowly makes her long arc across the sky and discover my own rising and falling. The moon will sing of quiet miracles, like those that reveal and conceal the world every day right before our eyes.

I crave a wide sea of wordless moments that allow me to express myself in another language, one more ancient and primal. I want to become a disciple of silence and hear in that shimmering soundlessness the voice of the One who whispers in stillness, whose singing vibrates in stones, who out of the silence calls forth a radical commitment of which I do not yet know the shape.

We emerge from the Earth matrix. The structures and rhythms of Earth are not external to our own thriving; rather, we arise from this holy sanctuary. It is vital to our own thriving. Creation as sacred space is the very foundation of our own existence.

Earth is that great biosphere which sustains our life moment by moment, providing oxygen and nourishment. We are woven into this Earth web, even though we may sometimes be tempted to view ourselves as separate from it, as objective observers rather than subjective participants.

David Abram, in his book *Becoming Animal: An Earthly Cosmology*, describes our connection with Earth this way:

> These planetary structures are not extrinsic to human life—they are not arbitrary or random aspects of a world we just happen to inhabit. Rather they are the constitutive powers that summoned

us into existence, and hence are the secret allies, the totemic guides, of all our actions. They are as much within us as they are around us; they compose the wider, deeper life of which our bodies are a part.[2]

The root of the word *matrix* comes from the Latin *mater*, which means "mother" or "womb." Like a womb, a matrix is a field out of which something emerges or is birthed. In this book, I begin with the assumption that Earth is the very matrix—the origin and sustaining environment—out of which our ability to care for ourselves emerges. Earth is the first place where we experience the kind of deep physical nourishment required for our bodies to thrive, but it is also a place of symbolic experience from which we derive meaning about our dependence on the Divine. A matrix is a place of grounding and birthing.

Merton's quote that begins this introduction is a keen reminder to everyone longing to experience a contemplative life to live the new creation now, not later or at another time. When we are committed to paying attention to this moment, we nurture our capacity to see the Holy active right here and now. We discover that the "kin-dom"[3] is among us now, and we live as if this were true. Thomas Merton believed that his one job as a monk was to maintain this kind of connection to the natural world, to allow it to be his teacher and guide.

We live in what we might call an age of forgetting. We have forgotten who we are in relation to everything else: the creatures, the plants, the mountains, the forests, the oceans, one another, and even ourselves. With every plastic we discard, with every poison we release on land and in water, with every fossil fuel extracted, we are living in the fog of amnesia. One of the fruits of contemplative practice is the remembrance of our wholeness; we are able to see past the divisions we create with our egos and minds and to rediscover the truth that we are all of one creation.

Douglas Christie, in his remarkable book *The Blue Sapphire of the Mind: Notes for a Contemplative Ecology*, describes the aim of contemplative living as addressing "the fragmentation and alienation that haunts existence at the deepest possible level and, through sustained practice, come to realize a different, more integrated way of being in the world.

Here, amidst the inevitable fragmentation of existence, the contemplative seeks to recover a vision of the whole and a new way of living in relationship to the whole."[4] This book is one attempt at this recovery; it is an invitation into remembering. Through practices and presence we can resurrect the memory of an ancient kinship. We are called to a holy remembrance of a wise knowing within us. We are not separate from nature and creation. We have animal bodies, and within us is a wild and intuitive capacity that goes beyond the carefully constructed plans we have for ourselves.

Christ and Creation

At the heart of the Christian tradition is the belief in the Incarnation, that God became flesh. This is expressed in a particular way through Jesus, but it also extends to all of creation. God did not become flesh for one time only; Jesus teaches us that the Divine Presence in all created things has been at work from the beginning of time and will continue to the end of time.

Jesuit theologian and paleontologist Pierre Teilhard de Chardin writes in his book *Divine Milieu*, "By virtue of the Creation and, still more, of the Incarnation, *nothing* here below *is profane* for those who know how to see."[5] God's inhabiting of the material world is as earthy as our spirituality can get, and yet we still have a lingering unease and ambivalence over the physical world as a legitimate site for connection with the Divine.

Jesus himself also demonstrates an intimate relationship to nature and the elements. John Klassen, O.S.B., writes in a reflection on environmental stewardship:

> Jesus shows a wonderful attitude toward created things by using water, bread, fish, wine, light, creatures such as birds of the air, foxes, seed and mud. The parables show that Jesus assumed the worth of the created universe, the dependability of nature, the recurrence of the seasons, the normal pattern of sowing and harvesting, of planting a vineyard and caring for it, of seeing the clouds and counting on the rain. The natural world is the stage

where the reign of God is enacted, the place where faith in God with all of its dimensions is lived out.[6]

The idea Klassen is beginning to describe is panentheism. The word *panentheism* comes from the Greek *pan* ("everything"), *en* ("in"), and *theos* ("God"). It means "God in all things, pervading everything we see" (this is different from *pantheism*, which means "all things are God"). While God is in all things, God is also wholly other; God is both immanent and transcendent. Jesus' embrace of the natural world reflects this panentheistic worldview.

Overview of the Book

In this book I have chosen to refer to "Earth" instead of "the earth." It is interesting that we refer to all of the other planets by names—Mars, Venus, Saturn, Jupiter, and so forth—but "the earth" is relegated to a lowercase reference. Often when we refer to nature, we are pointing to something beyond ourselves rather than acknowledging something we are a part of, woven into—the more-than-human world.

The overall theme of the book is that Earth is the original monastery, the original teacher of contemplative practice. Each chapter then breaks this initial image open by looking at a specific aspect of this theme, such as by exploring Earth as the original cathedral, original scriptures, original saints, original spiritual directors, original icon, original sacrament, and original liturgy.

Each chapter follows a similar pattern, beginning with a reflection on the overall theme and a story from one of the Christian saints that shows their kinship with creation, followed by a suggested practice and a scripture reflection written by my husband, John Valters Paintner. Then there is a series of explorations to deepen and integrate your experience of the theme, including a meditation, an invitation to go on a contemplative walk (see more below), working with herbs (see below also), a visual art exploration, and a writing exploration. Each chapter includes poems and prayers written by participants in online and live retreat offerings of this material, and each chapter closes with a blessing.

As with most of the books I write, I do not recommend just reading this book through from cover to cover. Each chapter is like a mini-retreat that could be worked through over a week or even a month's time. Many people work together on the chapters in small groups, meeting at regular intervals to share the process of discovery. I also offer online experiences on my website to support individuals wanting to work with others.

The order of the experiential explorations is a suggested sequence, moving from meditation, to contemplative walk, to working with herbs, to making visual art, and then to writing. But trust your own inclination and begin where you feel most drawn and inspired, while also making time for those explorations you feel resistance to trying for various reasons. We often learn the most about ourselves by dancing on those edge places between comfort and discomfort with gentleness.

The explorations are meant to be engaged slowly. You can take your time working through them, but I highly recommend you actually try them. Reading only takes us so far in our journeys of transformation. When we engage the world kinesthetically by being out in nature and paying attention, we have a different kind of encounter than we have with words on the page. The words of the world are intended to be your primary teacher, with this text as a support system for listening.

In addition, I work primarily through the expressive arts, in which process is more important than product and engaging in multiple modes of creativity has a way of breaking things open in new ways. Creating in partnership with creation ushers us into a deepened intimacy and way of seeing the world. All of the visual art explorations engage the materials of nature, poetry writing invites us into a different way of thinking, and working with herbs calls us to engage plants in a different way—one that honors them as allies and acknowledges their healing gifts in our lives.

Contemplative Walks

I encourage you to make time each day to be outside. One of the ways to do this is to go on a contemplative walk with an intentional and reverential heart.

There is something about getting our bodies out into the world, in close contact with trees, bushes, flowers, squirrels, pigeons, and crows, that can invigorate us and offer us new perspective on life. In the book of Jeremiah, God asks, "Do I not fill heaven and earth?" (Jer 23:24). These walks are times to really experience that truth.

Contemplative walking does not necessarily mean walking slowly, although at its heart it is not a rushed activity. When we walk contemplatively, we give ourselves over to the experience. This is not walking for fitness. It is walking to immerse ourselves in an encounter with whatever is calling us in the moment.

As you begin a contemplative walk, allow a few moments simply to breathe and connect to your heart. Set an intention for this time to be as present as you can to what is happening both within and without. Begin walking, but see if you can release any expectations or destination. As you walk, imagine that with each step your feet are both blessing the ground and being blessed by it. Let your breath be long and slow. Bring your awareness to the earth monastery all around you.

Notice what draws your attention. Look for what shimmers or what the Japanese poet Basho called "a glimpse of the underglimmer."[7] Listen for the sounds of life around you. Even if you are walking through a city, pay attention to the rustle of the breeze, the caw of crows, or any subtle elements of creation singing their song.

Pause regularly simply to receive this gift. Breathe it in. Let it have some space in your heart. Then continue on until something else causes you to stop.

This is the whole of the practice: simply walking, listening, and pausing. We practice presence so that we might cultivate our ability to really hear the voice of nature speaking to us. This sounds simple, and yet we so rarely make the time to develop this skill.

In each chapter I will have a suggestion for a contemplative walk with a particular focus to keep in mind that connects you to the chapter's theme more closely.

Working with Herbs

Over the last several years I have slowly been falling more and more in love with the beauty and power of herbs. This appreciation was first sparked when I encountered the writings of St. Hildegard of Bingen, the twelfth-century German Benedictine abbess and healer, while I was in graduate school, and she became a guide and mentor for me on the monastic and creative way. She was an herbalist herself, and the monasteries in the Middle Ages would all have been keepers of the traditional sacred medicine, with herb gardens at the center of their enclosures.

Moving to Ireland has brought many gifts to my life. I was interested in herbalism when I lived in Seattle and dabbled in it in small ways. Now I have studied with two wonderful herbalists near where I live, and the gifts of the plants are wondrous.

Perhaps the greatest gift is wandering the land with pilgrimage groups and in the spring finding nature's bounty available, including hawthorn blossoms, dandelions, daisies, primrose, plantain, nettle, and more. Autumn offers us sloe berries, elderberries, and hawthorn berries. It is a wonderful thing to create from them as gifts from Earth. I often try to create at least a tea or syrup of some sort to share with our group before the week's end as an incarnational experience of the gifts of this land.

I have started growing herb boxes on our patio in our Galway apartment as well; the first year was rosemary, oregano, thyme, sage, spearmint, chives, and lavender. They wintered well outside in the wind, so last summer I added lemon balm, mugwort, motherwort, and St. John's wort. This summer I now have yarrow, fennel, angelica, woodruff, and wild strawberries. I dry the leaves for teas, I bundle some herbs for incense, and I add them to baths.

You will be invited to work with plant materials in different ways, from incense, to ritual tea, to anointing oil, and more. I invite you to always begin from a place of wonder and gratitude, to see the plants as your allies, as supports on the spiritual journey, and as gifts of a generous Creator. You might call forth the spirit of St. Hildegard and all the monks throughout the ages who were keepers of this sacred medicine and healed both body and soul.

All the herbs used in this retreat are common and nourishing to the body, and they have been used for many hundreds (if not thousands) of years. Please check with your physician if you have any health conditions, take medication, or have concerns at all prior to using the herbal creations you are invited to make in this book.[8]

View of Wonder

So diverse are you, words cannot form the feelings of my soul
Passion Purple, Robust Rosemary, Holy Hyssop
All my senses feast in your gifts
Gifts for healing, arousal, comfort, and play
Lavender to comfort restless nights
Star-like seeds explode with joy
Humbly, I accept all you graciously offer

—Linda Smith

Falling in Love

In my book *Water, Wind, Earth, and Fire: The Christian Practice of Praying with the Elements*, I refer to a letter the Canadian Catholic Bishops published on our relationship and responsibility to Earth.[9] They described three primary paths—prophetic, ascetic, and contemplative.

The prophetic path asks us to work for justice, to change our ways of living that contribute to Earth's destruction, and to see the connection between poverty and pollution. The ascetic path asks us to discern how to live more simply and lightly on the planet, to reduce our use of plastics, pesticides, and fossil fuels. The contemplative path is the one I am called to focus on in my writing. In this path we cultivate intimacy with Earth and her creatures, and we allow ourselves to fall in love with nature. It is one of my deepest beliefs that we will not be able to address the environmental crisis we currently face without this intimacy, without learning how to cherish nature, without love.

Charles Eisenstein, a cultural commentator, observes:

Climate change portends a revolution in the relationship between nature and civilization, but this is not a revolution in the more efficient allocation of global resources in the program of endless growth. *It is a revolution of love.* It is to know the forests as sacred again, and the mangroves and the rivers, the mountains and the reefs, each and every one. It is to love them for their own beingness, and not merely to protect them because of their climate benefits.[10]

We need to claim the great wisdom and teachings the scriptures and mystics have to offer to us about remembering the sacredness of all things. We need to live an incarnational theology that takes God's presence seriously in all of creation. Only from this place of love will our hearts be transformed and a new way of being arise. This book is an invitation to fall in love with creation and see what is inspired from there.

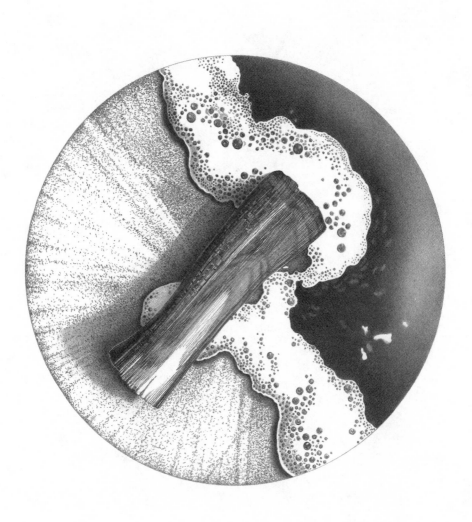

CHAPTER 1

EARTH AS THE ORIGINAL CATHEDRAL

It could be said that God's foot is so vast
that this entire earth is but a
field on God's
toe,

and all the forests in this world
came from the same root of just
a single hair
of God's.

What then is not a sanctuary?
Where then can I not kneel
and pray at a shrine
made holy by God's
presence?

—St. Catherine of Siena, "The Sanctuary"[1]

Sometimes when I work with retreat groups, I start by having them engage in a simple storytelling exercise called babbling,[2] in which retreatants pair up and each person speaks for a minute on a word I provide. It is a spontaneous activity, and the idea is to just notice what comes up in the moment. I might offer words like *lemon, mountain, wolf,* or *purple,* and people tell stories that arise in the moment. Then the last thing I ask participants to reflect on is a place that is a sanctuary for them. There is

1

often a shift of energy in the room as people describe their own sanctuary places, and the majority of people describe a place in nature.

Biologist Colin Tudge writes in his book about trees, "Groves of redwoods and beeches are often compared to the naves of great cathedrals: the silence; the green, filtered, numinous light. A single banyan, each with its multitude of trunks, is like a temple or mosque—a living colonnade. But the metaphor should be the other way around. The cathedrals and mosques emulate the trees. The trees are innately holy."[3] Next time you are in the forest, imagine this space as one of the primordial or original churches—a sanctuary that has helped inspire the creation of thousands of other sanctuary spaces. Notice what arises in your body when you imagine being in the cathedral of trees, joining them in praise of the Holy. Pause and slow down, aligning yourself with God's presence there. The cathedrals we build reflect the sacred spaces that trees have already been creating for thousands of years.

Some of the stories of St. Patrick tell us that he first learned to pray outside during his early years as a slave in Ireland and how his presence in the woods and the mountains summoned forth a continual stream of prayers in response to that sacred space. The Celtic tradition holds closely the idea of thin places, where heaven and earth touch. The landscape in Ireland where I live is dotted with hundreds of sacred spaces including holy wells, sacred mountains, and stone ruins.

St. Francis of Assisi is probably the saint that most often comes to mind when we consider how to connect to the beauty and solace of nature. His church was in the more-than-human world of nature that he loved so dearly: "Sometimes he preached by the candle-light of stars. Often the cloistering trees along the roadside made his chapel, and the blue sky was the only roof between him and heaven. Often his choir was of the brother birds in the branches and his congregation a group of brother beasts."[4]

Field and forests, mountains and shorelines became the site for St. Francis's worship and discovery of the intimacy of God. He is known for preaching to the birds and for the prayers he wrote that celebrate the gift of the natural elements.

Joachim of Fiore was a twelfth-century Cistercian mystic in Italy who likely influenced St. Francis. He is also known for worshipping outside.

It is said that sometimes when he was leading a service and the clouds cleared away, "he saluted the sun, sang the *Veni Creator*, and led the congregation forth to view the shining landscape."[5]

When we take Christ's Incarnation seriously, we discover that the Holy is indeed everywhere. Church spaces are beautiful and sacred, invoking the Sacred Presence and providing important places to gather. But nature offers us the original cathedrals and churches. When we step among trees with our eyes and hearts open, we discover the radiance to be found there. Jesuit paleontologist Pierre Teilhard de Chardin writes, "By means of all created things, without exception, the divine assails us, penetrates us, and molds us. We imagined it as distant and inaccessible, whereas in fact we live steeped in its burning layers. . . . The world, this palpable world, which we were wont to treat with the boredom and disrespect with which we habitually regard places with no sacred association for us, is in truth a holy place, and we did not know it."[6] The world we live in is "in truth a holy place," and our task is to remember this and to cultivate a growing awareness of the ways in which forest and hills can inspire a sense of sanctuary in our hearts. We would not desecrate our chapels and churches; in the same way, the more we nurture this intimate connection to Earth, the more we will be inspired to protect it at all costs.

Geobiographies and Archetypal Landscapes

Archetypal landscapes are spaces that are evocative and meaningful to people across cultures and time. Their existence acknowledges that we are shaped by the landscape we live in and that some landscapes speak to our hearts more clearly and resoundingly than others.

For some of us, it may be the forest that calls to us as the great cathedral of creation. For others, mountaintops are the pinnacle, offering an experience of spiritual transcendence. Or perhaps it is the sea that calls to your heart, offering her rhythm of pouring forth or drawing back, creating a temple out of its depths and hallowed ground at the rich space where sea meets earth.

Scripture is filled with holy encounters on top of mountains, in caves, and by lakes, rivers, and seas. Irish monks were inspired by the desert call to find solitude in wild places and journeyed out to the wilderness for an experience of radical intimacy with God.

One of the ways to connect more deeply and intimately with a felt sense of creation as the original sacred space is to remember the landscapes that have personal significance. Art therapist Peter London describes these as "geobiographies," the inner contours of the landscape of our souls:

> Each of the great forms that Earth takes—mountains and hills and plains and valleys and meadows and steppes and swamps and marshes and deserts and forests and jungles and savannas and beaches and islands—each of these geographies we transmute to geobiographies of our own personal journey across time and circumstance. We too rise up, we ascend, we fall, only to rise and fall over and over, until we are leveled and become one again with the single mantle that is the resting ground and birthing ground of it all. The meanings we ascribe to the trajectory of our lives are the same ones we observe in the fate of the Earth. The finite summit of the mountain's peak, the river's final arrival to the sea, the clearing in the depths of the woods, serve as exemplars and as metaphors for the often steep and uncertain and perilous journey that is our life.[7]

Earth has multiple terrains, as does the soul. Becoming familiar with the outer landscape reveals dimensions to us of our inner ones as well. Recognizing which territories enliven our souls and which ones challenge us brings us closer to discovering who we most deeply are and what we long for.

Mary Reynolds Thompson, in her book *Reclaiming the Wild Soul: How Earth's Landscapes Restore Us to Wholeness*, describes five archetypal landscapes she calls "soulscapes," which are the meeting point between the inner world of self and the outer world of Earth. These soulscapes are desert, forest, oceans and rivers, mountains, and grasslands.[8] Each landscape has a set of unique gifts and invitations, including the draw from simplicity to mystery, the flow of our desires, the power we have to inspire and shape the world, and the call to settle into a place and create community.

In my own life, I have found myself in love with particular places because of the way nature is alive there. I grew up in New York City, about as far from wild nature as you can get. However, my father was Austrian, and in the summers we would travel back to Austria to visit family and spend time in the Alps in the Tyrol region of western Austria.

We would often hike the trails in the Alps; I would try to keep up with my father as he walked in his measured pace and told me about the great Austrian writers, artists, and composers. Every so often I would ask him how much farther the trail was while pausing to catch my breath and admire the Alpine cows along the way that munched slowly on the grass. Sometimes he poured a bit of beer on a picnic bench, and I would giggle as the cow's great thick tongue came and lapped it up. Once we arrived at the trail's end, there was always a hut that served *knodelsuppe*, a rich beef broth with a large bread dumpling sitting in the center, often with *speck*, a kind of bacon. Hiking those trails had a kind of certainty to it: no matter how challenging, you always stayed on the path and would eventually reach the goal.

When John, my husband, and I were finishing up graduate school in the San Francisco Bay area, we visited a friend in Seattle, Washington, and we both fell in love with the Pacific Northwest. The landscape, with its intertwining of forest, sea, lake, and mountain, kindled something in our hearts we hadn't felt before—the land was calling to both of us. Over the nine years we lived there, I especially fell in love with the places where the wild edges meet—the borderland between forest and sea—and I discovered this place within me. We each have within us many threshold places where our love of the Divine meets our love of the world, where our hearts and minds unite, where the differing parts of ourselves come together to listen to our calling in the world.

When we moved to Vienna, Austria, from Seattle because of a call to adventure, the *Wienerwald* (Vienna woods) became a source of great solace for me as I dealt with the loneliness of living in a new place far away from my familiar life, and I deepened in my appreciation of the witness of trees. Now living on the west coast of Ireland, I am learning to love the rawness of this wild edge, the way the wind blows fiercely off the Atlantic, the haunting sound creating its own kind of church bell summoning my attention back to the current moment in time. In this place with few trees, stone has become vitally important for my sense of what it is that endures.

Think of the garden path or diving into the deep sea, of climbing majestic mountains or crossing wide open plains. Even walking through an urban neighborhood has its own kind of resonance. Each one has a particular quality that evokes something within us.

Pause for a moment and imagine each of these places, and allow a few moments simply to become aware of your body's physical response to a particular kind of landscape. Some may make your heart soar, while others make it contract; some may create no real felt response at all.

Beasts and Saints: Ross Errilly Friary

About a half-hour drive north of Galway City, in the west of Ireland, when you arrive at the village of Headford, you can turn left at the crossroads. Two kilometers down the road is the turn to visit Ross Errilly Friary, the ruin of a fourteenth-century Franciscan abbey. It is a beautiful site, one of the best-preserved medieval Christian monasteries in Ireland, with beautiful stone archways and the cloister walk fairly intact.

We bring our pilgrim groups. I have heard the beautiful stone ruins blanketing the Irish landscape sometimes called "sky-clad" churches because the roofs are mostly gone and they invite us into a unity of sky and earth at the heart of our prayer. Rather than think of these churches as ruins, we might consider the invitation rising up from these spaces to remember Earth as our original place of worship and encounter with the Divine. This is one of the things I love most about these old stone churches in Ireland: they invite us to hold the traditions of faith while also making connection with Earth, seeing the two as unified.

Theologian John Philip Newell describes the nunnery on the sacred island of Iona in Scotland as holding a similar kind of invitation to consider the sacredness of the stones while also feeling the connection with sky and earth. Because this monastery is a ruin, the roof is no more. It has a very different feel from praying in the abbey on the island, which has been rebuilt. Newell writes, "The desire to pray in the Nunnery is the desire to pray again in relationship with the earth."[9]

There is a story that says that at the time Ross Errilly Friary was founded, the bubonic plague was spreading rampantly and monks were ministering to those in need. Archbishop MacHugh prayed for the plague to end and his energy to be renewed. It is said he fell asleep while praying and had a dream in which he was instructed to build a church. He was told to walk west until a sign was given to him. He took three friars with him, and they set out. Eventually they saw three swans holding bunches of flax seed in their bills and flying overhead. The swans circled three times, and as the swans flew away, the monks drew closer to see the earth beneath where they circled. They found flax in full bloom, even though it was only February. This is where the church was founded.

There are many stories like this in the Christian tradition, especially from the desert and Celtic monks, in which connection to animals had a special status and significance and God could be found offering signs and guidance through their presence.

The Practice of Stability

Stability is one of the three vows Benedictine monks make. It is a commitment to a particular monastery for life. St. Benedict had special disdain for monks who would wander from place to place, because he knew well that when we try to outrun our issues in community, the issues will always follow us.

Benedict writes in his Rule that from the day of a monk's monastic vows, "he is no longer free to leave the monastery, nor to shake from his neck the yoke of the rule which, in the course of so prolonged a period of reflection, he was free to either reject or accept."[10] St. Benedict required his monks to commit to a monastery for their whole lives so that they would not run away when things got challenging.

Stability calls us to a commitment to work through the difficult things of our lives. We can run away both physically and emotionally in our desires for distraction, entertainment, and ease. When we are in a long-term relationship with another person or with a community, there will be times of challenge and times of boredom. The monastic way is to stay with this commitment and see what we are taught in the act of staying through the discomfort. This is the work of a lifetime.

There is another aspect to the practice of stability, and that is commitment to a place. When we vow to stay and work through the challenges we feel, we are deepening our relationship not only with those we share a life with but also with the landscape that shapes us and the creatures and plants that inhabit our region. Stability also calls us to grow in our love of the particularity of the place where we live, the particular cathedral we inhabit. We are invited to learn the names of the birds that visit or the herbs that grow up in the cracks and fields.

When we move often from place to place, it is challenging to deepen into our commitment to the land we are living on. Recognizing Earth as our original sanctuary means deepening our love for the ground that nourishes us at home as well as away. It means finding the spots nearby where we can sit and ponder and be with nature in all her splendor, even if that is a bench in a city park. Deepen your commitment to learning about the place you live—the local birds, plants, animals. Finding out their names roots us more strongly in place.

Scripture Reflection from John Valters Paintner

The First Creation Myth (Genesis 1:1–2:4)

In the beginning when God created the heavens and the earth, the earth was a formless void and darkness covered the face of the deep, while a wind from God swept over the face of the waters. Then God said, "Let there be. . . ."

—Genesis 1:1-3

There are two separate creation myths in the book of Genesis, and they contradict each other significantly on the timing and order of events. Most scholars agree that the second myth actually predates the first. The two common responses to this conundrum in the opening chapters of the Bible are either to dig in one's dogmatic heels and insist that it's all factually literal or to throw it all out as a bunch of made-up ancient folklore that is neither scientific nor historical and therefore irrelevant to modernity.

Fortunately, there is a third approach. What the two previous approaches get wrong is in understanding what is meant by "inspiration." When we say the Bible is "inspired by God," that isn't to say that God dictated stories to people but rather that people were compelled to write stories about their encounters and understanding and—perhaps most importantly—even questions about God. Myths aren't "made-up stories"; they are tales that point to greater truths.

What sets the creation myths of the Judeo-Christian sacred texts apart from others of the ancient Middle East is not the belief in monotheism (although that is revealed slowly over time to the Israelites). No, what is unique about that new religion was the belief in a different type of deity, a belief in a good and benevolent God. Other ancient cultures believed that the world was a cruel and chaotic place. They believed that, at best, the gods ignored them. They believed the world was full of suffering and death because that is how they viewed their gods. These ancient religions prayed and sacrificed in hopes of appeasing the petty and greedy natures of their gods.

The ancient Israelites, however, looked at the same world and saw a good and bountiful world. The first creation myth in Genesis is a theological statement of their belief that God created order and beauty and abundance out of the chaos. Our spiritual ancestors prayed and sacrificed to thank God for what they had already been blessed with. The second creation myth explains why there is suffering and death in this good and perfect world. Hint: it's not God's fault. Combined, the two myths work as a type of prelude to the "main event" of the Hebrew Scriptures: the Babylonian Exile. They foreshadow the establishment and then destruction of the Israelite kingdom.

In the first creation myth, God does not create something out of nothing. There is something before the creation. There is a formless void, a swirling storm of wind and water unfit for human life—an analogy of the fickle Babylonian storm god Ba'al (a recurring foe to Yahweh and the Israelites throughout the Hebrew Scriptures). What God does is to slowly, methodically, and very intentionally create order out of the chaos. The Israelites' God speaks, and the Babylonians' god obeys. The analogy is carried over into the Christian scriptures when Jesus orders the stormy sea to be calm.

Over the course of the six days of the first creation myth, God builds a protective bubble that keeps the waters above and below at bay. God dries the land within and plants vegetation there. God then sets up the days and seasons to regulate and organize the world. Next, God creates animal life to fill the world. Finally, as a culmination of all the preparation, God creates humans (man and woman together on the same day) in the divine image.

And it was very good.

Although it avoids the "dominion" language of the second creation myth, the first is understandably human-centric: all the world and all the plants and animals therein are created for the purpose of sustaining human life. This perspective is off-kilter, but after all, the scriptures were written by human authors for a human audience, neither of which were much concerned with objectivity at the time. God created the world for God's own delight, blessing all aspects of the world as good apart from their usefulness for humans. But there is another lesson in the first creation myth to be learned as well. All of creation is the intentional handiwork of the Creator. Not just humans but all of creation mirrors the beauty of the Creator. Nature is experienced as a vast and sacred landscape shimmering with goodness because of its divine creation. Nature is the original sacred space and sanctuary where humans are invited to dwell.

While some read Genesis and interpret it to mean that we humans are better than creation, the proper interpretation is that we humans are part of creation. We are connected to all life through our common Creator. We may have more responsibility, but we do not have greater status.

Meditation: *Lectio Divina* with Nature

If creation is a visible revelation of the Divine Presence in our midst, then we might consider it worthy of prayer and contemplation. We can bring the practice of *lectio divina*—or sacred reading, where we sit with the words of scripture and listen for a word that shimmers or calls to us, let it unfold in our imagination, receive the invitation, and then bask in silence—to this other "book" of revelation available to us.

Make time for a slow and contemplative walk in nature. As you walk, imagine yourself to be in a great cathedral of trees, stone, and sky. Listen for a word nature offers to you; it might be the song of a bird, the rustling of leaves, the silence of stones, or the sea drawing out on the tide. You might be reminded of a familiar phrase, or a new one may be evoked. This "word" becomes a catalyst for your own inner reflection and experience, sparking memories, feelings, or images, allowing space for these to unfold.

Then you open to an invitation that emerges from this prayer of listening. It is a call from Earth to a deepened awareness—to rest in silence and simply to savor it all, knowing that you are ultimately called simply to rest into being rather than doing. Perhaps you find yourself in conversation with nature and discover you are not talking to something separate but you are woven into this matrix of life.

Philosopher David Abram writes that "prayer, in its most ancient and elemental sense, consists simply in speaking *to* things—to a maple grove, to a flock of crows, to the rising wind—rather than merely *about* things."[11] This is an invitation to understand prayer as deeply incarnational, discovering the presence of the Holy woven through every element, so that we no longer address our prayers to some transcendent being but are right in conversation with the shimmering immanent presence of the Divine through every leaf, acorn, gust of wind, and mossy stone.

Theologian Belden Lane calls this sacred reading of nature *lectio ter-restris*.[12] The practice is simply to notice what is calling your attention, reflecting on what you are drawn to, listening for the invitation arising from this, and then sitting with your prayer in silence.

Contemplative Walk: Participation in the Life of Creation

See if you can bring your contemplative presence to creation to an even deeper level of participation. Find a place where you can experience a connection to creation, such as a nearby wooded area or park. Begin by walking around this space in the way you normally would with a contemplative awareness and openness. Perhaps you move between listening to the world and pondering your own life journey. Maybe you feel a subtle separation between yourself and the world due to discomfort or judgment.

Now take off your shoes and socks and stand barefoot on the ground. (If it is midwinter with freezing temperatures, adapt this for your own needs.) Allow some time to connect to the ground beneath you. Deepen your breathing; as you inhale, imagine drawing up energy from the earth through your feet and up your legs. As you exhale, imagine sending down deep roots that will draw nourishment. Notice the temperature of the earth, the texture, the resistance or yielding of the ground. Walk a few steps and become fully present to the way the ground feels as you move across it.

Then kneel down if you are able and feel the earth in your fingers. Adapt as needed. Bring all of your senses to this experience, noticing texture, smell, sounds around you, any taste arising in your mouth, what the earth looks like. Let yourself play for a little while. What might you have done as a child? How might your exploration have been more free and spontaneous? See if you can let that part of yourself have some time to explore.

Look around you and explore the texture of tree barks, the feeling of plants between your fingers, their smell.

Open yourself to the sounds around you. Rather than reaching for sound, simply receive whatever it is you hear. When sounds do arise, notice them and let them go. There is no straining in this exploration, just an openness to experience.

Then open yourself to the spirit and wisdom of this place. See if you might experience yourself connected to this earth, these trees, these flowers, woven together with them. Feel your relationship to the insects crawling under the ground or in the trees.

Open your heart as much as you can to receive other levels of awareness beyond your five senses. See if you can let go of trying to have a specific kind of experience, and simply sense yourself being here without agenda or goals. How is Earth a cathedral for you?

Notice what your experience is like now. Rest in this space as long as you desire, and see what you discover.

Herbal Invitation: Ritual Tea

A ritual tea is a cup of tea you drink slowly and with intention. Tea is one of the simplest ways to work with herbs and a beautiful way to engage with God's gifts of healing plants. You might already drink herbal teas regularly. I invite you to let this be a contemplative and full-sensory experience. There is magic for me in pouring hot water over the plant materials and being present to the scent that arises, the color that infuses the water, the warmth of the mug. I pause as the herbs steep in the water; I wait to sip until the water cools. St. Hildegard of Bingen, known for her book on herbal medicine, would most certainly have regularly sipped healing herbs in tea form, so we can connect to her spirit as well through this action.

Begin by turning off any distractions, such as your phone, email, TV, or radio. You might choose to play some sacred music such as sacred chant or classical music. Be intentional about your choice, and know that silence is also entirely welcome.

Choose the herbs you want to drink. Peppermint is a lovely choice, and it's easy to find and can support digestion. Many people like chamomile to drink in the evening to help relax. If you'd prefer something fruity, hibiscus is a good choice and has a high vitamin C content. Place your herbs into a pot or a special cup. You can use a tea infuser, a strainer, or a reusable tea bag in which you place the herbs and fold it to hold the herbs in. You will want to put one teaspoon of herbs into your pot or cup per one cup of boiling water. Offer gratitude for this offering from Earth for your own healing journey.

If you don't have herbs, for this experience you can work with any herbal tea you might already have at home or that is easy to buy at the local supermarket. If you have a box of peppermint tea at home, a blend of herbs, or even a green or black tea, you can move through this experience of making and drinking the tea as a prayer.

After choosing your herbs or tea, continue with some deep breathing to drop your awareness out of your mind and thoughts and down into your heart center. Let yourself experience the herbs from a heart-centered place of receiving what gifts might come. Release any need to figure out what anything might mean, and gently quiet your mind when it tells you there are things waiting on your to-do list.

This is a meditative act. As you fill your kettle from the tap, imagine the waters arriving from the rain that falls and the rivers that flow. Bless the water as it boils. Breathe deeply in the quiet moments. Bless the fire that heats the water, even if the source is electric.

Once the water boils, pour the water over the herbs and savor the steam that rises. Watch the herbs dance and bring their color to the water. Close your eyes for a few moments as the tea begins to steep. Breathe and pause and listen. Imagine the heat of the water breaking open the goodness of the plant material to make it available to you to drink. Feel the warmth of the cup; smell the fragrance as it rises. Savor this moment with nowhere else to be.

After a few minutes, once the herbs have steeped and the water cooled enough to drink, you can bring your tea to your lips for the first sip. Drink a small amount, feeling it in your mouth, tasting the flavor, then swallowing it and imagining the way it moves through your body systems to bring nourishment.

Bring your awareness to this exploration of Earth as the original cathedral. Imagine this ritual tea is an act of communion with creation, celebrating the gifts of healing and nourishment Earth offers. Give gratitude to God for any special places of sanctuary that restore and renew you.

Continue drinking the tea in this way. Continue to savor each sip and this time of stillness and reflection.

Visual Art Exploration: Building Cairns

Study the Stone

Be yourself. And if what this means
is unclear to you, look around at

the things of this earth. Study the stone
which always does what it was made

to do: it doesn't always fall in the
same way, sometimes resting in high

places and at other times finding its
rest where the earth allows it to lie,

but its purpose is to move downward,
and in this the stone loves God in the

way it can, singing the new song
which God gives each creature and thing—

and also you who read this and at times
wonder what to do and how to be.

—Meister Eckhart[13]

I invite you to go for a walk where your intention is to collect stones out in nature—in the woods, at a river or beach, from a park—and place them on your altar. If you don't have a home altar yet, consider making a small space somewhere you can put a cloth, a candle, and some symbols from nature. Home altars help to connect us to the Sacred in our everyday lives. Take some time to hold each one and get in touch with their shape and texture. Stack them one on top of another to create a cairn, which is a Gaelic word for a human-made pile of stones that serves as a landmark,

often marking the top of a mountain or a burial site. They indicate something sacred nearby.

You might also create cairns along a familiar and favorite nature trail
as a way of marking sacred points for you. Allow the stones to signify
your own heart's response to the physical space.

Written Exploration: Nature Walk with Haiku

Haiku is a wonderful form of concise poetry traditionally written about
nature. Writing haiku invites you to focus on the essence of your experience because the first line is only five syllables, the second line is seven
syllables, and the third line is five syllables. Try writing one or more haiku
in response to your prayer experience this week. You don't have to hold rig-
idly to the syllable count; just try to express things as concisely as possible.
Allow the poem to lead you to what feels most essential to remember. I find
that the more I write these, the more I fall into their rhythm.

Previous Participant Poems

Wind blows through the pine
The river runs by the stone
Robin finds her meal.

—Ann Dissek

sister tree laughing
sing your dream alive calls bird
sea dance tickling toes

—JoAnn Heiser

Diamonds sparkle
On green pine tree needles, light
Sprouts, winter's delight

—Jenny Meyers

Closing Blessing

Earth offers us the original sacred space. Many of us already find solace and inspiration in outdoor settings. This first chapter invites us to consider even more intentionally, as an act of love and reverence, the way God is revealed through creation.

Each chapter ends with a blessing written by one of our program participants to support you in celebrating nature's gifts. Allow the words of someone who has already taken the journey you are now on to serve as a guide and companion for you.

> May the song of the birds be the bearer of your joy.
> May the softness of the moss be the pillow for your dreams.
> May the puzzle of the monkey bring adventure to your steps.
> May the down of the feather be the gentleness of your touch.
> May the wild nettle grove be the healing of your pain.
> May the tiny petals falling awaken wonder in your eyes.
> May the gold of buttercup reflect the deepening of your love.

—Valerie Allen

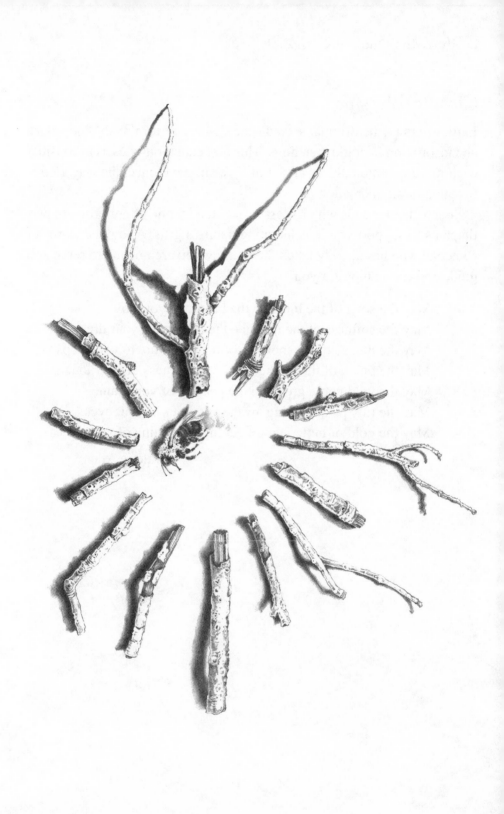

CHAPTER 2

EARTH AS THE ORIGINAL SCRIPTURES

Believe me, you will find more lessons in the woods than in
books. Trees and stones will teach you what you cannot learn
from masters.

St. Bernard of Clairvaux[1]

The Celtic Christian tradition maintains that we receive two books of
revelation. One is the book of the scripture texts, and the other is the vast
book of creation. We need both to receive the fullness of divine wisdom.
The ninth-century Irish theologian John Scotus Eriugena, who empha-
sized the immanence of God, wrote in his *Homily on the Prologue to the
Gospel of John*: "For the divine knowledge cannot be restored in us ex-
cept by the letters of scripture and the sight of creatures. Learn the words
of scripture and understand their meaning in your soul; there you will
discover the Word. Know the forms and beauty of sensible things by your
physical senses, and see there the Word of God."[2]

The words of scripture offer us one kind of insight into God's Word,
and the physical dimension offers another. God is in all things and is the
true essence of all things. One of Eriugena's favorite words is *theophany*,
which means "something that reveals the divine nature." For him, the
world and all of creation is a theophany.

Remember a time when you were in a place of great natural beauty
and the elements were speaking to you in some way. Perhaps through the
wind blowing you found you were able to release something you were

clinging to, or maybe flowers were blooming and you realized there was a new bud growing in your own heart. Maybe you stood at the edge of the vast expanse of sea and felt the grace of your smallness, a welcome sense of humility in the greatness of the whole world. Remember how the divine nature was revealed to you at that moment.

John Howard Griffin, who went to live in Thomas Merton's hermitage after Merton's death, kept a journal of his time there. In it he wrote, "The very nature of your solitude involves you in union with the prayers of the wind in the trees, the movement of the stars, the feeding of the birds in the fields, the building of the anthills. You witness the creator and attend to him in all his creation."[3] Presence to the first "book" of revelation brings us again and again back to the heart of the Divine. To witness creation as a sacred act is to come to know God as the Great Artist more intimately.

St. Anthony the Great, one of the earliest desert monks, was asked once by a visitor how such a wise man coped in the desert without any books. Anthony replied, "My book is the nature of created things, and as often as I have a mind to read the words of God, it is at my hand."[4]

Spend some time imagining the world around you as a sacred book full of the wisdom you need to navigate through life in meaningful ways. The seasons, the elements, the creatures, the landscape, and the weather all dance together to offer us a revelation of the Holy Source of all that is.

The Seasons Are Our Scripture Text

When we pay attention to the rhythm of the seasons, we learn a great deal about the rise and fall of life, about emptiness and fullness. Spring invites us to blossom forth; summer calls us to our own ripening; autumn demands that we release and let go; and winter quietly whispers to us to rest, to sink into the dark fertile space of unknowing, to release the demands of productivity and calendars and to-do lists, and simply to be. Jesus' life was attuned to the necessary rhythms of serving and retreating for rest. He preceded the initiation of his ministry by taking forty days in the wilderness, and he arose early before light to find some time in solitude to pray before beginning to preach (see Mt 4:1–17; Mk 1:35–39). What grace we could offer our bodies by living according to these rhythms! In

the winter seasons of the body, we might fully allow the fallowness needed to restore our souls to fruitful ground. The fifteenth-century Indian
mystic and poet Kabir recognized that "when eyes and ears are open even
leaves on the trees teach us like Scripture."[5]

When you bring your attention to something in nature, whether a tree
or a stone or a creature, and bring yourself fully present to it, you can
sense its inner stillness, meeting a place of stillness in your own heart.
You can experience how much it rests in the great Being who holds all of
us, with no divisions, and in that awareness you discover that place within
you as well. Theologian Sharon Therese Zayac writes, "Thomas Aquinas
tells us that 'Sacred writings are bound into two volumes, that of creation
and that of Holy Scripture.' He speaks of creation first because creation is
the primary revelation. We came to know God in creation long before we
met God in scripture."[6] I love this image of Earth as original scripture; it
is the first text we meet long before we encounter the holy books.

When my mother died in October 2003, I was plunged into the heart
of grief, a most unwelcome journey at the time. It was my daily walks
among the trees that offered me the most solace. Most people wanted to
offer words to explain or help me understand or move on from my grief.
The trees stood in silent witness and simply followed their own natural
unfolding, becoming radiant with brilliant reds, yellows, and oranges as
a spectacle of surrender. The leaves slowly released their hold on the
branches and sometimes were shaken free by autumn winds. I walked for
hours among those trees as they slowly grew more bare, returning to their
essence, and I found them so beautiful. Winter's sparseness reflected back
to me my own inner reality. It was during this time that I fell in love with
winter and the gifts she offers. "What is it the season for?" a wise spiritual
director used to ask me, inviting me to tend to my inner seasons as well as
the outer one unfolding around me. She knew that nature's wisdom could
offer me guidance and grace.

By the following spring, I was not quite ready for an inner blossoming; that would have to wait at least another year. But I had felt held; I
had read the wisdom of the scriptures dancing around me and heard my
grief honored.

St. Melangell and the Hare

There is a wonderful story about St. Melangell, a sixth-century woman originally from Ireland who wanted to flee her impending marriage and so went to Wales to live as a hermit. She lived there for many years, when one day a group of hunters with their dogs were chasing a rabbit across the fields. The rabbit was chased to the hermitage where St. Melangell was living and jumped into her cloak for protection. The hunters and dogs were unable to approach. The prince was with them and was so impressed by this woman's presence that he offered her the gift of all the land surrounding her hermitage. She said she would receive it only if it could be a place of sanctuary for any animal in danger.

This is a powerful story of how a creature's wise knowing revealed to the prince the desire of God: that Melangell would have a safe place for all. When we pay attention to what nature offers to us, rather than to what our own agendas are, our hearts might be transformed.

There is to this day a chapel in that valley in remembrance of Melangell, and the place is still considered a sanctuary. We are called to seek the wild spaces of our lives, to break free from the places that feel confining but also to find places of sanctuary where we are offered the gift of rest and safety. From there we can find nourishment to return again and again to the wild edges and hear nature as scripture verse.

The Practices of Wonder, Enchantment, and Astonishment

It is easy to become disengaged with the world around us. Sometimes the onslaught of terrible news greeting us each day is enough to make us retreat under the covers. In her book *The Enchanted Life*, Sharon Blackie writes:

> Ultimately, to live an enchanted life is to pick up the pieces of our bruised and battered psyches, and to offer them the nourishment they long for. It is to be challenged, to be awakened, to be gripped and shaken to the core by the extraordinary which lies at the heart of the ordinary. Above all, to live an enchanted life

is to fall in love with the world all over again. This is an active choice, a leap of faith which is necessary not just for our own sakes, but for the sake of the wide, wild Earth in whose being and becoming we are so profoundly and beautifully entangled.[7]

Practicing enchantment is a commitment to seeing the world through new eyes. It means shaking off our cynicism and numbness and rediscovering the world that shimmers behind the everyday.

Theologian Steven Chase, in his book *Nature as Spiritual Practice,*[8] describes developing the capacity for astonishment as a primary spiritual practice. We don't earn transcendent moments in nature. There is nothing we do to deserve a wide night sky with a thousand glittering points above. No accomplishment earns the sun rising above the sea in shades of violet, fuchsia, and amber. The only proper response to these transcendent moments is to bow our heads in gratitude and to join in the prayer already at work around us.

While we will certainly explore in this book the necessary path of grieving and lament for the destruction of nature, an equally essential approach to nature is to cultivate our sense of wonder, enchantment, and astonishment as an act of resistance in an age of cynicism and despair. Only then might we be able to read the scriptures around us and hear what they are saying. They will help to guide the way.

Scripture Reflection
from John Valters Paintner

The Temptation of Jesus in the Wilderness (Luke 4:1–13)

Jesus, full of the Holy Spirit, returned from the Jordan and was led by the Spirit in the wilderness, where for forty days he was tempted by the devil. He ate nothing at all during those days, and when they were over, he was famished. The devil said to him, "If you are the Son of God, command this stone to

> become a loaf of bread." Jesus answered him, "It is written, 'One
> does not live by bread alone.'"
>
> —Luke 4:1-4

This passage is usually associated with Lent, a time of preparation for
Easter. However, I am going to begin with Christmas. Luke's infancy
narrative starts with two miraculous pregnancies: that of Mary, a virgin,
and that of her cousin Elizabeth, long thought barren and past childbear-
ing years. Luke writes of angels and heavenly messages. He tells of surprised parents-to-be and infants dancing for joy. There are two different
canticles, songs of joy sung by Mary and Zechariah. And just when things
couldn't get more special, angels appear again and welcome shepherds
to visit the child Jesus as a sign that this new king is for even the lowly
commoner. Luke then gives us a glimpse into Jesus' early life with an account of when, at just the age of twelve, the future Messiah stays behind
in the Temple in Jerusalem and amazes even the chief priests with his vast
wisdom and teaching at such a young age.

Luke doesn't leave much room for the reader to see Jesus as anything
less than a great spiritual leader. Even before Jesus begins his public ministry, all signs point to his divine nature and special role in salvation history.
But before that public ministry can begin, we have Jesus' time in the desert.

Luke's version of the temptation of Jesus in the desert comes at an
odd time in the narrative. John the Baptist has announced the coming of
the Messiah, and Jesus has just been baptized by John and anointed by
the Holy Spirit at the Jordan (with the presence of a dove and voice from
heaven). Luke then painstakingly gives a genealogy that traces Jesus'
ancestry back through King David and the patriarch Abraham to Adam
himself. All of this is to lay out who Jesus is, where his authority comes
from, and what he has been sent to do.

But first, Jesus goes on retreat—for more than a month.

Why, after thirty years (during a time in history when life expectancy
was about the same age), did Jesus wait another forty days to begin his
public ministry? Where did he go and what was he doing for so long that
was so important?

Nothing. That's the answer. Jesus wasn't even eating. And when the devil arrives toward the end of those forty days, Jesus takes no action. Jesus just speaks, quoting some scripture.

"Nothing," however, isn't a completely accurate answer. Jesus may not have been doing anything; yet, he was being. He sought out the wilderness so he could make time to read the first "book" of creation.

This is one of the lessons that Jesus gives through his example: before action, contemplation must take place.

And for true contemplation to happen, one must step outside oneself. We have to get outside the noise and confusion and chaos that surround us, that we create around ourselves. Jesus very intentionally goes out into the wilderness, out into God's nature, in order to find space for contemplation. Just as we might read scriptural text before we make a significant decision, we might also read the original scriptures, creation, as a source of wisdom and solace before the next season of life. Spending time reading the original scriptures helps us also to remember the need to step back, to truly rest and contemplate before we rush into action.

Meditation: Praying in Rhythm

There is such tremendous wisdom to be learned from the simple act of paying attention to the rhythms and seasons of nature that embrace us. There is wisdom in allowing them to be a doorway into our own deeply felt experience and allowing ourselves times of rest alongside fruitful activity throughout the day.

There is the early morning threshold of dawn when Earth begins to awaken and birds join together in song inviting us into the morning prayer of Lauds.

Then comes the brilliance of a sunlit midday, when the monks would pray Sext, and we feel the fullness of life burgeoning forth.

This is followed by the gentle descent of evening and the threshold of dusk, the time of Vespers, when crows gather together in trees to announce the coming of the night. We leave behind the unfinished tasks of the day.

And the day closes with the hour of midnight and the deep darkness of nature's silence. We are invited into mystery and unknowing and to acknowledge the reality of our eventual death and final sleep.

Merton wrote often about how the forest opened up in him the monastic way of praying. Night is the hour of Compline, when monks enter into the great silence. The trees have much to teach us about entering into the great and beautiful mystery of evening. Night also opens us up to our radical state of unknowing, the reality of grief, and the need for lament.

Your invitation for this meditation is simply to set an alarm (a gentle chime on your phone would be ideal) for the times of dawn, midday, dusk, and bedtime. These specific times will vary according to the season, but that is part of the practice—to become present to the changing windows of light and dark. At each of these moments in time, pause for a minute of silence. Become present to the invitation of this time, and listen for what it calls you to consider. Dawn might ask you what you are awakening to. Midday may ask what in your life longs for illumination. Dusk might ask what you are called to release. And dark may ask you to open yourself to mystery, to live into the questions of life rather than to seek answers. Consider these hinges as scripture texts, offering their own sense of direction and purpose.

Contemplative Walk: Paying Attention to the Signs of the Season

Before you head out for a contemplative walk, allow a few deep breaths to bring you to your own sacred center. Drop your awareness from your head, the place of analyzing and planning, and into your heart, where you can receive each moment with wonder as a gift. You aren't trying to make anything happen during this time. You are showing up with eyes and ears attuned to the presence of the Spirit in the world around you. Call to mind the season you are in. Hold this as an awareness and intention for your walk, allowing nature to show you signs of the season and receiving them as a sacred text.

As you take each step during your walk, listen to where your attention is being drawn. Notice the leaves on the ground, the bark of the trees, the sparrow singing, a rose blooming out of season. Approach the world in a spirit of mutuality, where the things of the world have things to say to you as much as you to them. When something "shimmers" for you—when something catches your attention in some way—pause with it and spend some time cultivating a relationship with it. See what this thing has to say to you. What wisdom does it want to offer about your life? How does it speak of the Divine Presence in all things? What if you considered it to be an offering of holy scripture?

This is the whole of the practice: To walk and be present. To breathe deeply and keep returning to this moment now. To honor what is calling you and spend some time listening to nature's gifts and what she offers to you. See if there might be a gift you can carry back with you—whether an object from nature or a moment when you might receive the gift of an image with your camera—and spend some time with it in wonder.

Once you return home, consider spending some time writing about your experience in a journal. Reflect on what you noticed and discovered. What is the original scripture revealing to you?

Herbal Invitation: Sacred Bathing

Water is a central ritual element in many traditions. In the Christian tradition, baptism and blessings with holy water are powerful experiences of renewal. Jesus washed the feet of his disciples. In Jewish tradition, the *mikvah* is a ritual bath to purify, renew, and cleanse.

You are invited to work with herbs in a foot bath. You can also do a full-body bath if you prefer, but just soaking your feet is a wonderful and healing treat and is sometimes easier to access. You can use any kind of loose herbs for this process, but marigold (calendula) is especially good for the skin. You can also use a couple of herbal tea bags if that is all you have available.

You will need a bucket or small tub that you can place your feet into. Even two deep pans would work. Boil about two cups of hot water, and pour it into the bucket; then add the dried or fresh herb you have chosen, and let it steep for about eight to ten minutes. Essentially you are creating a very strong herbal tea and drawing out the plant's properties. Then add warm water to fill the tub so that the temperature is comfortable and you can submerge your feet. If you have sea salt or Epsom salt, you could also add a handful of the salt to increase the relaxing qualities of the foot bath.

If you would prefer not to have the loose herbs in the tub with your feet or worry about emptying them out in the sink, you can create a strong tea first by using a tea infuser in a mug and then pouring the tea into your tub.

As you prepare the water and pour in the herbs, hold awareness of the source of both the water and the herbs. Imagine the great rains that fall and bring us water, and imagine the fields of flowers and plants dancing in the breeze.

Pause and offer a prayer for this time. In this moment, you are offering yourself a tender act of self-care. What in your life right now could use some healing? Some slowing down and pausing for reflection? What, if healed, would create space for the fullness of your own light to shine forth? Call on whatever you need for support. Ask that the waters and the herbs be blessed by the presence of the Spirit at work.

Dip your feet into the waters slowly, savoring the warmth as it surrounds you. Take three slow, deep breaths, and notice if there is any place in your body that needs softening. Bring some breath there.

As your feet soak in the tub, imagine your connection with Earth through this communion with the herbs. Call in the grounding support of the soil that grew the flowers, and ask for grounding and what you need for growth in your own life. Call in the brightening inspiration of the sun that brought the flowers into their full radiance. Call in the nourishing waters of rain that helped grow the herbs to flow to the dry and arid places in your life. Imagine that each aspect of this experience is a scripture text with holy wisdom to offer.

Notice how your body feels as you continue to soak, relax, and release. Allow a full ten to fifteen minutes to rest and soak. Offer gratitude to your feet for all the miles they have traveled.

When you are done, carefully dry your feet with reverence. You may want to slather on some cream or oil as a way of anointing and giving thanks for how they carry you through the world. Give thanks to the herbs and their gifts of healing and renewal.

You might spend a few more minutes in quiet after the experience noticing what stirred for you, especially whether taking time for self-care was welcome or challenging. Simply notice without judgment, and perhaps allow some time to journal and make note of what you discovered.

Visual Art Exploration: Contemplative Photography

The visual exploration for this chapter can be done in conjunction with the contemplative walk described earlier in this chapter. In it, you were invited to go for a walk in nature where you pay attention to the signs of the season. To make this walk a visual art exploration, bring your camera with you; it can be as simple as your phone camera.

In my book *Eyes of the Heart: Photography as a Contemplative Practice*,[9] I write about the difference between "taking" photos and "receiving" them. The first is reflective of the consumerist, grasping, scarcity-focused mindset that is so prevalent in Western culture. The second is the call of the contemplative, the one in us who sees all of life as gift and so receives the graces offered with a sense of wonder and gratitude. Pay attention to what gifts and graces arrive when you move through the world in an openhearted way. The frame of the camera lens helps you to see them in new ways and reflect again later on what you have encountered. If you notice yourself grasping and trying to "capture" as many images as you can, pause and breathe deeply. See if you might soften into the moment and shift your awareness to receiving images as gifts.

When you return home, allow some time to be with the images received. Notice which images especially shimmer for you, and consider them to be a holy text. You might journal about anything that is sparked in you.

Writing Exploration: Ways of Circles of Response

This writing exercise is adapted from the work of Mary Reynolds Thompson and Kate Thompson in *Environmental Expressive Therapies*.[10]

To begin, think about something in nature you have had an encounter with during the last week, perhaps something you found on your contemplative walk. Spend a few moments breathing deeply and reflecting back on this last season, and see what comes to mind. Then, allow about five minutes of free writing for each of these three reflections:

1. How does this make you feel? What aspect of your life does this reflect?
2. How might you learn to speak the language of this thing from nature? Pause after this free writing and see if anything surprised you.
3. Take this thing you were drawn to and bring it inside of you. Write: *The [thing] in me knows . . .* and then keep writing to explore your response. Again pause after this free writing to see what surprised you.

This is an exercise in becoming aware of the egoic circle (reflection one), the ecological circle (reflection two), and the cosmological circle (reflection three). These are three different ways of interacting with and responding to nature. The egoic circle refers to our own private feelings and experiences. The ecological circle is the bridge from the inner to the outer world, where we see ourselves in relationship to nature or the place we are in. The cosmological circle embraces everything that has ever existed and connects to a sense of transcendence. This is where our deepest sense of belonging to the cosmos is kindled. We come to know ourselves as intertwined and interwoven with everything else, and the separation falls away. Suddenly all of creation is seen as a source of revelation, as the original scripture.

Previous Participant Poems

By Grace Alone

How is it you do it,
Little sandpiper?
How is it you live
By grace alone?

For you it is true,
Knowing God provides.
I see,
You never doubt this.

And when it's time
You willingly surrender:
Your hallowed body
Ravaged through with ants.

How is it you do it,
Little sandpiper?
How is it to live
By faith alone?

—Ivette Ebaen

The wave in me knows . . .
I have a purpose, a destination, and a gift
There is time to rest and roil in the deep
And a time to engage in the journey
I am part of a greater calling
A community of others
Carrying forward the deep things of God
Not to hoard but give
A journey full of risks
Persevering
Changed by what I have no control over
Impacted by the forces of nature and others
Tossed about by the waves of time
Moving a few steps forward
At times losing ground
Then carried onward by the strength of another
Clinging to the shore
Sparkling like a diamond in the warmth of the sun
Living into the ebb and flow of life.

—Linda Holmes

Reflection One: How does this make you feel? What aspect of your life does this reflect? I am drawn now, as I was at the beginning, to my beautiful wreath. She has kindly allowed me to rest on the warmer side of my door, while reminding me that nature awaits! Hibernation is healing, and exploration invigorating.

Reflection Two: How might you learn to speak the language of this thing from nature? I learn to speak the language of the wreath in knowing that life is not a straight line. We are always beginning again.

Reflection Three: Take this thing you were drawn to and bring it inside of you. Write: The [thing] in me knows . . . and then keep writing to explore your response. The wreath in me knows that life is here to be discovered at my own glorious pace.

—Bridget O'Grady

~ morning moon setting ~
feeling ~ one with ~ moon (self) always present, seen and unseen

language of ~ beyond words, reflective ~ gentle, strong, fierce, calm, true ~
the moon in me knows ~ true self whole, free, wonder, sadness and solace, love and mystery ~ true to own nature ~ authentic in its being ~

the moon in me knows ~

—JoAnn Heiser

Closing Blessing

In this chapter you have been invited to consider the ways Earth is the original scripture. How might paying attention to the rhythm of the days and the seasons offer you wisdom about how to move more gently through your life? What graces does an honoring of dusk and night, as well as autumn and winter, offer when lived into as a balance to our spring-and-summer culture?

Thank you for the generosity of
birds who sing their celebration
of life without ceasing—
may their chirps, tweets, twitters, coos, and hoots
continue to bless the land.

Thank you for the wild rhododendrons
who don their lovely purple frocks each spring -
dancing with delight in the gentle breeze
and dotting the landscape with color.

Thank you for the busily buzzing bees
who do the important work of pollinating
to ensure the continued fruitfulness of the earth.

Thank you for the grandeur of trees
that provide a canopy from the rain and sun
and stand as majestic, silent witnesses
to the blooming, buzzing, chirping world.

Praise be to God for all
of these wondrous things.

—Carol Scott-Kassner

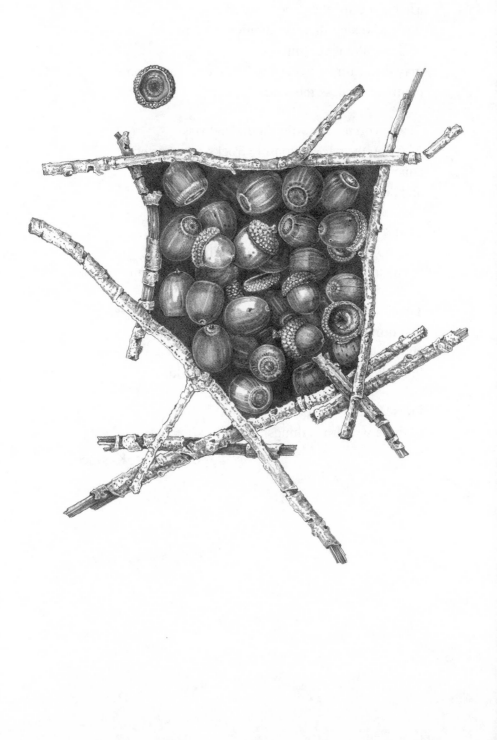

CHAPTER 3

EARTH AS THE ORIGINAL SAINTS

The pale flowers of the dogwood outside this window are saints . . . the bass and trout hiding in the deep pools of the river are canonized by their beauty and their strength. The lakes hidden among the hills are saints, and the sea too is a saint who praises God without interruption in her majestic dance.

—Thomas Merton, *New Seeds of Contemplation*[1]

The poet David Whyte has a beautiful line in his poem "What to Remember When Waking" where he asks, "Why are we the one terrible part of creation privileged to refuse our own flowering?"[2] He is calling us to awareness. Imagine that everything created was formed with this natural impulse or instinct toward its own flowering into fullness. Why do we, as human beings, work so hard to resist our calling?

After the quote that begins this chapter, Thomas Merton goes on to write: "For me to be a saint means to be myself. Therefore the problem of sanctity and salvation is in fact the problem of finding out who I am and of discovering my true self. Trees and animals have no problem. God makes them what they are without consulting them, and they are perfectly satisfied. With us it is different. God leaves us free to be whatever we like. We can be ourselves or not, as we please. We are at liberty to be real, or to be unreal. We may be true or false, the choice is ours."[3] The animals don't spend time in discernment; the trees don't go off on retreat to listen to their calling. They simply are exactly as they were created to be, and in that simple witness, they reveal a path of yielding, of not resisting, and of simply allowing themselves to unfold as intended.

We need time in silence, away from the distractions of daily life. We need guides who can help us to identify and celebrate our gifts. We need wise ones who can help us identify our shadow material—those places of resistance and refusal to be who we are most called to be.

The animals and the elements live their fullness without holding back, and in them, we can discover what it truly means to become a saint, to be fully ourselves, as Merton writes. The trees and flowers do not try to be other than they were created to be. They teach us how to live out our own sainthood by no longer refusing our true nature. To become a saint means to embrace our essential nature, which is the vessel through which we carry out our callings. Mechtild of Magdeburg, a thirteenth-century German mystic and member of the Beguine movement, wrote, "The truly wise person kneels at the feet of all creatures and is not afraid to endure the mockery of others."[4]

Merton says that to be a saint means to be myself. This sounds so simple. And yet, we know how challenging it is, how many obstacles we set before ourselves, how many layers of fear and resistance have built up over the years, how much our egos are attached to being viewed in a certain way, and how tight we hold on to certain images and identities.

As you sit with these words from Merton, I invite you to listen for this call to be fully yourself and to listen for how best to get out of your own way. Let your heart soften into suppleness, readying yourself to receive a new insight, a new vision. Listen for the wisdom that arises in the stillness, and then share it with your community.

This feels so challenging—in fact, it's a lifelong journey. Here is the wisdom Merton offers to us: To be fully human means to live in connection to nature and receive her wisdom and guidance. To live among the trees and the rhythm of sun and moon, to see the rise and fall of the tides and the strength of mountain presence, is to slowly feel these things within us. To recognize them as teachers and mentors provides inspiration for how to follow this path of authenticity for ourselves. Creation is the original sainthood, the witness to what it means to be fully oneself without forcing or holding back.

To become a saint doesn't mean to be some contrived image of holiness, practicing your faith in ways that imitate others. It means finding
your own unique expression in the world, the seed that was planted within
you when you were born. You are a revelation of the Sacred, and there is
only one revelation just like you. Nature can help you to claim and live
into this truth.

Animals as the Original Monks

There is a story about St. Ciaran, one of the early Irish monks, in which
he encounters a wild boar who was made tame by God: "That boar was
St. Ciaran's first disciple or monk, as one might say, in that place. For
straightway that boar, as the man of God watched, began with great vigor
tearing down twigs and grass with his teeth to build him a little cell."
After the boar built himself a cell, other animals came from their dens to
accompany St. Ciaran, "and they obeyed the saint's word in all things, as
if they had been his monks."[5]

I love this image of the animals as St. Ciaran's first monks. I love
that they formed his original community. One of the great delights of the
desert and Celtic monastic tradition is the abundance of stories of saints'
special connection to animals as a sign of their holiness.

The Gift of Sourney

Our canine companion Sourney arrived into our lives in early February
2018 at Imbolc, which is the Celtic season of the very first sign of spring
and also the feast of St. Brigid. The previous three years John and I had
fostered dogs over the Christmas holiday when the public shelters in Ireland close down and the rescue groups are overwhelmed with the number
of dogs that need care. That year we both had come down with a terrible
flu over Christmas, but by the end of January, when we started to feel better and recover our energy, we realized we had missed our annual dose of
canine energy and so contacted the rescue group to see if any dog needed
some extra care or help.

They got back to us quickly. Chime, a Patterdale terrier, had been
with them for many months, and they thought she could use a break from

kennel life. After we went to pick her up and bring her home, we quickly realized that her name, Chime, was not easy to say or remember. She was such a quiet girl, so we decided to name her Sourney after a local woman saint whom we have very little details about other than two sacred sites. Our new companion's ears seemed to perk up at her new name, and so it stuck.

As the weeks went by and she settled into life in our home, I realized she was a special dog, especially well-suited to our lives—she was very quiet and mellow, loved to sleep in each morning, was a super snuggler, but also loved a good walk each day that got us outside. When we sent in photos to the rescue group to post to generate interest in her, I felt hesitant. Even though it wasn't the best time of our lives to adopt a dog, as we travel so much for work, it felt as if perhaps we should now consider having a dog full time in our lives again.

We adopted her, and I have been so grateful to have canine energy in our home once more. The rhythms of sleep, food, and going out for long walks feel very grounding for us as city dwellers. She is a faithful presence, loving nothing more than to be with her humans. If I had operated on my assumptions about how we didn't have time to have a dog in our lives right now, I would have missed out on her great gifts of love and affection sustaining me in this season of my life. She is a source of daily wonder and delight and a reminder of what it means to follow one's path each day. Sourney doesn't try to be other than she is, and she doesn't struggle with doubts. Instead, she is fully and beautifully *dog* and, as such, a perfect witness to grace. She witnesses to what being a saint means.

St. Francis and the Grasshopper

There is a lovely little story about St. Francis of Assisi that tells of a winter night when the snow was tumbling down all around the monastery. Francis's brother monks were all tucked into their warm beds, and when time came for night prayer, none of them got up, preferring the comfort of sleep.

St. Francis arrived to the chapel. With no one else there, he sat in prayer alone. After a short while the door opened, and in came his friend, a grasshopper, to join him for night prayers.

I love this story of Francis's intimacy with creation and how a creature showed up to support him in prayer on a snowy night. This story reminds me of the truth of how having animal companions can be a sign of a holy life. I am reminded of the psalms that tell us how all of creation is already singing glory to God. There is a sense of wonder in this story—in the heart of a dark and cold night, possibilities still erupted into that space.

The Practice of Gratitude

The fifth-century Italian monk and mystic St. Benedict of Nursia counsels in his Rule for monastic life an attitude of contentment among his community. Whatever the circumstances they find themselves in, Benedictines are to find some satisfaction with what is in the moment. In a world of self-entitlement and inflated sense of need, learning to be content with what we have has the potential to be quite revolutionary. It means craving less and being more satisfied with what one has.

One way to encourage this posture of contentment in our lives is gratitude. Gratitude is a way of being in the world that does not assume we are owed anything, and the fact that we have something at all—our lives, breath, families, friends, shelter, laughter, or other simple pleasures—is cause for celebration. We can cultivate a way of being in the world that treats all these things as gifts, knowing none of us deserves particular graces.

We might begin each day simply with an expression of gratitude for the most basic of gifts—life itself. We can awaken each morning with gratitude for another day to live and love, grateful for our breath and a body that allows us to move through our day. Then we can offer gratitude for a home and all the things that are important to us about this place of shelter. Gratitude is a way for us to cultivate a healthy asceticism and to reject consumerism.

Gratitude is a practice that can begin with the smallest acknowledgment and be expanded out to every facet of our existence. A simple way to nurture this awareness in our lives is to end each day with a gratitude list. You might write five to ten things for which you feel grateful each day, lifting up both the large and the small moments of grace. It is a way to end the day by honoring the gifts we have received rather than dwelling on where life came up short for us. Consider saving these notes of your grateful awareness together somewhere, in a journal or on slips of paper in a jar, and after a season of time, read back over the things that made your heart expand. Notice what patterns you find there.

Gratitude has a way of transforming our approach to life into one that is more openhearted, generous, and joyful. Rather than moving through our days feeling cynical or burdened, we can consciously choose our thoughts. This doesn't mean that we have to offer gratitude for injustices or abuse; we are always called to resist those. But it does mean we might be able to tap into greater joy to replenish ourselves for those moments when we do need to fight for dignity and kindness. Gratitude overflows into joy and makes us feel connected to something bigger than ourselves.

When we engage in gratitude as a regular way of being, we are living in a way that recognizes that everything is gift. Br. David Steindl-Rast, a Benedictine monk, has a book that has been very meaningful to both John and myself: *Gratefulness, The Heart of Prayer: An Approach to Life in Fullness*.[6] In it, Br. David invites us into gratitude as a way of life, one that sees life as abundant. Gratitude is a beautiful way to cultivate our own "saintliness," to live in such a way that we honor the gifts we have and let go of our striving for things beyond our reach. Gratitude can lead to a deep sense of peace and equanimity in our lives.

Barb Morris, a participant in one of our online retreats exploring this material, writes:

> To be in gratitude is to be vulnerable, to be expanded, to be opened, to be shown my dependence on others—other creatures, other people, and Earth herself. To be grateful is to bow to my interwovenness with all Creation.
>
> And anything can happen out here where we're all open and available to each other. Where I'm exposed to my weakness and need for your strength and gifts. Where I'm not pretending to be

entire and sufficient unto myself. Where I'm food for the wolf and the grizzly, and I eat the deer and the thimbleberry. I drink the river's water, and the trees breathe my breath. I share my molecules with stars.

So that's how I think gratitude is a wilding practice—when I'm grateful and courageous, rather than grasping and fearful, I open myself to the entities with which I share this beauty-full Earth, upon whom I depend for my life. Gratitude unlocks our cages, sets us free from our straight-lined lives, so we can meet each other, change each other, make all things new together.[7]

Scripture Reflection
from John Valters Paintner

Do Not Worry (Matthew 6:25–31)

Therefore I tell you, do not worry about your life, what you will eat or what you will drink, or about your body, what you will wear. Is not life more than food, and the body more than clothing? Look at the birds of the air; they neither sow nor reap nor gather into barns, and yet your heavenly Father feeds them. Are you not of more value than they? And can any of you by worrying add a single hour to your span of life? And why do you worry about clothing? Consider the lilies of the field, how they grow; they neither toil nor spin, yet I tell you, even Solomon in all his glory was not clothed like one of these. But if God so clothes the grass of the field, which is alive today and tomorrow is thrown into the oven, will he not much more clothe you—you of little faith? Therefore do not worry, saying, "What will we eat?" or "What will we drink?" or "What will we wear?"

–Matthew 6:25-31

Matthew's gospel, while not being the shortest of the gospels, certainly doesn't waste much time getting into Jesus' preaching. By the end of chapter 4, Jesus' genealogy has been given; he's been born, visited by magi, escaped to Egypt, and returned; he's been baptized by his cousin John in the Jordan; he's spent forty days in the wilderness, begun his public ministry, and called his first disciples; and he is now drawing big crowds.

The pace and tone of Matthew's account change slightly with the beginning of chapter 5, where we get the first of Jesus' actual preaching. Jesus covers a variety of topics, starting with the Sermon on the Mount and the Beatitudes. Chapters 6 and 7 are full of teachings in quick succession, including an example of how to pray with what becomes known as the Lord's Prayer. There's a lot to take in, from new laws or commandments, to teachings on sexual matters, to oaths, to almsgiving, to fasting (just to name a few).

But among all these heavy, spiritual matters is a comforting new instruction: don't worry. Jesus doesn't suggest that we worry less or encourage us to try our best not to worry. Instead, he says, *Don't worry.*

Easier said than done, right? Of course it is. However, Matthew's Jesus gives us examples of our fellow creation that do not worry—and are all the better for it. The birds of the air and the lilies of the field are those whom we humans should look to as an example. These are the original saints.

The implication of this new commandment certainly is not that food, clothing, and shelter aren't important. The implication is to trust in the Creator, as does the rest of creation. It is to avoid being so anxious about the little things in life that we ignore or overlook the bigger picture. The rest of creation, by design, finds balance. Only we humans are so worried about our survival that we horde and destroy.

How might we better follow the example set by the winged angels we can see and the heavenly paradise we touch? How might the sparrows be a witness to what sainthood really means?

Meditation: Resting in Gratitude

This meditation can be done any time of day, but it might be especially meaningful at the end of each day as a way to reflect back on the events and encounters of your day with a heart of gratitude.

Find a comfortable seated position, and spend some time deepening your breath and bringing your awareness to your heart center. As you breathe in, imagine your heart expanding to behold the gifts of your life. As you breathe out, release any worries or concerns you carry for the moment.

Begin by remembering your ancestors, both of blood and of spirit, whose lives have inspired your own, whose labors meant that you were given the gift of life. Call present this cloud of witnesses. Offer gratitude for their presence.

Remember the people of your life who bring you joy and comfort, beginning with those closest to you—friends and family, neighbors and coworkers—then moving outward and thinking of the people who work to deliver your mail, remove the trash, work at the grocery store, or smile at you at the bank: all those who bring ease to your daily life in various ways. Then widen that out further and breathe in gratitude for all people and cultures across the globe trying to make the world a better place.

Remember the gifts of the earth and the sea, the creatures who inhabit them, and the plants that offer their nourishment. Call to mind any places in nature that are sanctuaries for you. If you have any companion animals, hold them with gratitude.

Remember the gift of life and all the ways you are nourished and sustained each day through shelter and food, through health and community, and through the wisdom of others, all the while holding a heart of gratitude.

Call to mind and heart the communion of saints, both those humans who have walked Earth and left their wisdom behind for us and the animals and other creatures whose presence inspires us to live more fully as ourselves.

Invite the presence of the Holy Spirit with you and notice how it has been moving in your life lately. Take time to name moments of inspiration and guidance.

Allow yourself to bask in this sense of gratitude for a while, and see what other images come. Who or what else sparks this heart-expanding sense of thanksgiving for you?

As you come to a close of this prayer, you might spend some time writing down a list of what you are grateful for and anything that arose in your prayer that surprised you. You are also invited to write your own prayer of gratitude.

Contemplative Walk: Walking in Gratitude

You are invited again to go on a contemplative walk. This time as you walk out in the world, keep a heart of gratitude open to what you encounter. You might begin with gratitude for your feet and the ability to walk or for your eyes and the ability to see. Then you could move on to the home you live in and offer gratitude for shelter.

As you move through your neighborhood, pause regularly to give thanks for the trees, the birds, the cat who passes you by, the breeze blowing, the sun shining or rain falling, your neighbors, the local shop—anything that inspires a sense of gratitude in your heart. You might even offer a small bow of reverence at each one to embody the thankfulness you feel. When you return home again, allow some time for journaling and writing down anything you noticed or discovered.

Herbal Invitation: Mugwort Dream Pillow

Mugwort is one of the sacred herbs in the Celtic tradition. It was also called cronewort, and it was considered to hold the wisdom of the crone (woman elder). Mugwort was also known for eliciting dreams. Dreams have a way of supporting us in calling forth our true self. Dreams help to illuminate our shadow places and the things we are holding on to that do not serve us. Dreams can guide us toward our own sainthood. Dreams were regarded as special messengers from God in the scriptures and the lives of the early saints; often, dreams sparked significant and transformative journeys in the lives of people who experienced them.

Bring a sense of prayerful presence to this experience and ask blessings on your dreamtime, that insight might be offered to you to help you move toward greater holiness and integration. Give thanks for the gift of mugwort, and ask that it gives you powerful dreams that lead you toward truth.

Find a small cloth bag that can be closed. In a mindful and loving way, add the mugwort inside the cloth bag. You could also add other herbs that support sleep in a gentle way, such as lavender, lemon balm, or rose petals. Close the bag and bless it as you place it either in your bed (inside your pillowcase) or on the nightstand beside you.

When you go to sleep at night, call on the support of the herbs to help you remember your dreams, and ask that your dreams may offer you guidance, insight, and healing. Ask that they help you to remember how to become fully yourself.

Visual Art Exploration: Working with the Materials of Creation

On one of your contemplative walks, become aware of any materials along your path that could be used as materials for your own creation—stones, sticks, leaves, or flowers. See if you can use found materials rather than breaking things off branches or stems. Earth offers up plenty of organic material to the great compost of life.

Let this be a contemplative experience, paying attention for which objects shimmer for you, what seems to hold wisdom or meaning or stories.

Once you have gathered enough materials, find a place to pause and enter into a time of creation. Arrange leaves into a mandala, create a nature altar, or engage in whatever form of expression you most desire to enter into.

Release the thinking, judging mind as much as possible. When thoughts do enter in, simply notice them, let them go, and return to your task. Let your creative process flow like the river until it arrives where it is going.

Ask the stones where they want to be laid; have a conversation with the twigs and leaves about how they want to be in relationship to one another. If the whole idea of talking to your materials makes you feel foolish, embrace the foolishness, and remember that this is about prayer and play and taking yourself less seriously.

When you have arrived at your destination—when there is a feeling of satisfaction with what has been created—simply sit with it for a while. Just notice your own experience. What do you discover as creator? How do you experience this kind of co-creation with the natural world?

You might want to receive this creation with a photo. Or you might not. Check in to see whether a photo feels like a helpful reminder of this moment or too grasping, too much like checking off an assignment or trying to create something permanent rather than allowing yourself an experience. Trust whatever emerges in response. Thank the materials for their invitation to you to participate with them in creating more beauty.

Then walk away. Practice humility and surrender by knowing that the organic nature of things means that this creation will eventually disintegrate back to the earth rather than be forever captured in the great halls of a museum. Like the Buddhist monks who create intricate mandalas from colored sand and then blow all the sand away, see if you can practice non-attachment, and be compassionate with any resistance you experience, just noticing it as good food for reflection.

Writing Exploration: Go to the Pine

The seventeenth-century Japanese poet Matsuo Basho offers this sage advice: "Go to the pine if you want to learn about the pine, or to the bamboo if you want to learn about the bamboo."[8]

Go to an element in nature, whether a tree, plant, stone, feather, or other object that shimmers for you today. Perhaps it is a companion animal in your home. Spend some time with it, listening to it, asking it to teach you about itself. Then write a poem about how you imagine this being experiences the world through all of its senses. What happens when you enter into its experience and listen? What are the barriers between yourself and the world that you could let down for a while? What is the poem that emerges from that space?

Previous Participant Poems

Oriental Poppies

The poppies in the church yard are getting ready to shout.
I wait for that sound every spring—
the magical moment when swelling buds
spill their intoxicating color into the church yard.
Waving like red Pentecost
banners, the poppies call me to join their celebration.
I can hear the poppies.
Coming closer, at
first I see only the fiery color of burning sun.
It reminds me of the story of Moses and the
burning bush.
It's then that I notice
beyond that color into velvet darkness.

It's not what I expected.
My gaze
touches a longing that holds me there for a long time.
Much later I leave
my damp sandals on the porch and walk barefoot into the house.

—Ellen Ratmeyer

Common Loon

There is nothing common here.
Incense is rising from the
lake. The lake is sacred.
Air is altar-ing,
reverberant, a primeval wolven wail.

The familiar tremolo, laid on
the brittle bone, makes hallowed with loon song.
The lake becomes a satin
bed sheet made for slipping into.
Submerging, cleanly stealth,
into a liquid underworld,
his tuxedoed slide and
surfacing, in distant,
silken silhouette, is an
event-horizon.

—Denice Bezoplenko

Leaves

Gently awakened by the sweet kiss of sap rising,
Slowly unfolding tender newness to the elements,
Glorying in the gift of light lavished by the sun,
Rustling songs of praise in every moment's breeze,
Gracefully releasing hold into a joyful dance of death,
Sweetly born anew in the humble humus of forest floor.

—Sharon Handy

Closing Blessing

In this chapter you have been invited to consider Earth as the original saints and how creation might be a witness for how to live into the full flowering of our lives. What are the internal obstacles and blocks you place in your way? What are the stories you tell yourself? How might the animals, even a companion one at home, help to teach you what it means to claim your own sainthood?

May a divine blessing rest on this blue wooden gate
and the rose-fragrant walled garden within.
May the songbirds be blessed
as they raise their canticles of praise.

Blessings be to you, O pond,
as you lift water to the sky as mirror.
Profusion held in perfection, meadow of life
may blessings attend you.
May your wattled walls provide divine illumination
for all pilgrims at the labyrinth's center.
Honeybee, may your diligent work be sweet.

—Carol Shatford

CHAPTER 4

EARTH AS THE ORIGINAL SPIRITUAL DIRECTORS

I was sad one day and went for a walk;
I sat in a field.

A rabbit noticed my condition and
came near.

It often does not take more than that to help at times—

to just be close to creatures who
are so full of knowing,
so full of love,
that they don't
—chat,

they just gaze with
their
marvelous understanding.

—St. John of the Cross, "A Rabbit Noticed My Condition"[1]

In the tradition of both the desert and the Celtic monks, having a spiritual director or soul friend was considered essential to the spiritual life. A wise guide and mentor can help remind us of our heart's true desires and how to live with more integrity.

In Christian tradition, there were often holy men and women who were described as having a special relationship to animals. St. Benedict, for example, befriended a crow who was later said to have saved his life from being poisoned. It was said of St. Kevin that an otter would bring him salmon every day from the lake so he could eat. These special connections and relationships to animals were once a sign of holiness. The animals, as well as other aspects of creation, often acted as soul friends to the monks and mystics.

We are called to live the life of the new creation in which right relationship to all creation is restored. We are not anticipating its arrival but living its becoming. The journey we are on now is the journey home, the journey to no longer live in exile from our physicality but to live the new creation in this moment which honors our bodies and the great body of Earth as essential vessels of wisdom.

We might be tempted to think that creation cannot speak to us in language and so it has nothing of importance to say. Rather than speak about nature, we might consider addressing our speech to creatures, knowing that they will respond in their own form of communication.

How much do we assume we know about the lives of animals, oceans, trees, or the wind? How much does this assumed knowledge obscure our capacity to enter into loving relationship with these beings and receive their wisdom? The monastic practice of humility is an invitation to allow others to offer us wisdom, to recognize that we don't always have the answer ourselves. The root of the word *humility* is *humus*, which means "of the earth." To be humble as a monk means to be profoundly earthy and grounded, to remember from where we arise and to where we return.

Nature has a way of offering us solace at times of need. I know I have many times walked in the woods while my heart felt heavy with grief. Being among trees has helped to lift something within me.

The Irish monk St. Columbanus taught the precept, "If you want to know the Creator, understand created things." He was known to "call the beasts and the birds to him as he walked, and they would come straightaway, rejoicing and gambolling around him in great delight. . . . He would summon a squirrel from the tree tops and let it climb all over him, and from time to time its head might be seen peeping through the folds of his robes."[2]

This kind of intimacy with nature means that when our hearts feel heavy or conflicted, we might find ourselves walking a trail in the woods, along a river, or in a nearby park to experience a sense of kinship with creation. In these moments, the natural world often meets us as a guide and offers insight or peace to us.

The Elements Are Our Spiritual Directors

How necessary it is for monks to work in the fields, in the sun, in the mud, in the clay, in the wind: these are our spiritual directors and our novice-masters.

−Thomas Merton, *The Sign of Jonas*[3]

Merton knew that the true mentor of the soul was nature itself. The fields, sun, mud, clay, wind, forests, sky, earth, and water are all companions for our own inner journeys. The elements of water, wind, earth, and fire offer us wisdom and guidance. They are the original soul friends. Air is the gift of breath we receive in each moment, the rhythm of life that sustains us. Fire is the gift of life force and energy, and we might call to mind St. John of the Cross's image of God as the living flame of love that burns in each of our hearts. Water is the gift of renewal and replenishment, and we might call to mind the ritual of baptism as a call to claim our full gifts, or the blood that flows through our veins. Earth is the gift of groundedness and nourishment. The bread and wine at the Communion table emerge from the earth; the act of eating is sacred and holy, and it sustains our life and work.

Ikkyu, a fifteenth-century Zen Buddhist monk and poet, writes, "Every day, priests minutely examine the Law and endlessly chant complicated sutras. Before doing that, though, they should learn how to read the love letters sent by the wind and rain, the snow and moon."[4] What a beautiful image to receive the gifts of creation as love letters written to us! It reminds me of how many of the great saints would write letters of spiritual direction to those who sought their guidance.

What would it mean to listen into the deep wisdom of these four elements for our own spiritual direction and guidance in life? Nature offers us this universal language with which to understand our own inner movements.

The twentieth-century Jesuit theologian and paleontologist Pierre Teilhard de Chardin writes that "by means of all created things, without exception, the divine assails us, penetrates us, and molds us."[5] *All* created things await to serve the divine purpose in our lives. There is nothing in nature that falls outside these parameters. Through every rock, every bird, every flower, and every creature, God enters into intimacy and communion with us. This is how God's wisdom is revealed, and we would do well to listen for their spiritual direction.

Befriending the Wind

John and I first moved to Ireland at the end of December 2012, in the heart of midwinter. I knew the wind was strong here, especially in the west buffeted by the Atlantic Ocean. Having lived in Seattle, I thought moving to another rainy climate would not be an issue, as I love the rain. But I wasn't quite prepared for the force of the wind in the winter months. The rain is much heavier here than in Seattle, and the wind often blows it sideways, what the Irish call "lashing."

I love my daily walks, and that first winter we were drawn to walk regularly along the Promenade, which is a three-mile walkway along Galway Bay. It is a beautiful walk on most days, but the wind is fierce right down by the sea, especially in winter. I would feel every muscle in my body tense up as we tried to walk into the wind, making every step an effort. I resisted the wind so much, was so frustrated by how hard it made walking. When I heard the wind howl outside the window, I felt a growing sense of dread.

Ireland is a very elemental place. Galway is surrounded by water on all sides with canals, the river, and the sea. Rain can be heavy at times and continues through most of the year. Stone is a significant element of the landscape with limestone to the south and granite to the west. The sun brings its welcome fire, often coming after a heavy rain and illuminating the pavement and wet grass in the fields. I had a love for each of these elements; only the wind felt like my enemy.

As the months passed I was grateful that the wind softened a bit in spring, summer, and fall. The following winter I braced myself for the fierce blowing again. But this time I began to soften myself intentionally as I walked. I stopped resisting and slowly began to appreciate the way wind can blow things free. When my mind is working especially hard at something, there is nothing like a good walk in the wind to help me release my grasp.

The wind has become a teacher of the power of the elements through my own invitation to meet it with a loving welcome, to allow it to do its work on me, as a good spiritual director can.

St. Kevin and the Blackbird

One of my favorite stories of the Irish saints is that of St. Kevin, who prayed each day with arms outstretched to God. One day, as he knelt in devotion, hands upheld to the sky, he felt a blackbird land on his palm and lay an egg there. It is said he was so moved that "in all patience and gentleness he remained, neither closing nor withdrawing his hand: but until the young ones were fully hatched he held it out unwearied, shaping it for the purpose."[6]

I love this image of Kevin opening his palm to the heavens so that new life can land there. Rather than withdraw his hand out of discomfort or because it wasn't in his plans, he yields himself to this invitation and becomes a part of the divine creative unfolding. He softens his grasp on how he thinks life should unfold and opens himself up to what is actually happening, making a space of welcome for it.

This is the heart of spiritual direction: to listen to the call that is arriving in our lives, not staying focused on some other self-conceived goal. A soul friend can help us to hold the space to listen and can invite us into our growing edges, the places we might otherwise pull back from.

The Practice of Mutuality and Reverence

The ancient monks used to practice a kind of inner and outer watchfulness. The desert mothers and fathers wrote about this frequently, for a central part of their spiritual discipline was to show up for life and pay attention. This kind of presence can be challenging in our modern world when our attention is pulled in so many different directions, but presence is a gift we can offer to another.

Cultivating contemplative presence to the natural world means growing in intimacy with creation so that the intimacy becomes a way of mutuality, in which we recognize that nature is not just there for our benefit but has intrinsic value apart from us and our needs. Mutuality means that we listen to what nature has to say to us. We allow our hearts to be opened by our encounters there.

When we practice watchfulness, we become aware of the wonder that surrounds us. Walking the path of wonder is a radical act in a world numbed by cynicism and despair. Trusting that holy surprises await us each moment if we only pay attention is a practice worth cultivating. In the coming days, notice when your thoughts start to tell a story of predictability, of knowing how things will turn out, or of trying to control the outcome. Practice wonder and presence to the world; listen deeply to her whispers.

Reverence is about seeing the Sacred in something. We practice reverence with nature when we honor the ways she reveals the Divine Presence to us. We offer reverence when we acknowledge the inherent dignity of something without concern for how it will serve us.

When we bring a sense of reverence to the natural world, we can't help but be open to grief as well as joy. The joy arises from beauty and presence; the grief is our sadness and perhaps sense of helplessness in the face of species becoming extinct, plastic clogging our oceans, the pollution of rivers and streams, the acceleration of climate change, and much more.

Scripture Reflection
from John Valters Paintner

Elijah Meets God at Horeb (1 Kings 19:9–13)

He said, "Go out and stand on the mountain before the
LORD, for the LORD is about to pass by." Now there was a great
wind, so strong that it was splitting mountains and breaking
rocks in pieces before the LORD, but the LORD was not in the
wind; and after the wind an earthquake, but the LORD was not
in the earthquake; and after the earthquake a fire, but the LORD
was not in the fire; and after the fire a sound of sheer silence.
When Elijah heard it, he wrapped his face in his mantle and
went out and stood at the entrance of the cave. Then there
came a voice to him that said, "What are you doing here,
Elijah?"

–1 Kings 19:11-13

This is perhaps my favorite passage from the Hebrew Scriptures. But before we get into Elijah's experience in the wilderness, we'll need a bit of a running start to catch up to him on the mountaintop.

This particular biblical story really begins a couple of chapters back in 1 Kings 17, when the prophet Elijah correctly predicts a great drought in the Holy Land as a result of the wicked reign of King Ahab and Queen Jezebel. (Just a quick warning against trying to equate modern natural disasters with stories such as this from the Old Testament: In these stories, the scripture authors are relating a specific case of the people suffering as the result of the unfaithfulness to the covenant and injustice toward the people by a particular ruler; they are not trying to establish a precedent whereby all future natural disasters across the globe can be attributed to the same cause. That kind of bad theology is a very dangerous type of spiritual appropriation.) God sends Elijah to the east of the Jordan River to a wadi, where there is water to drink and ravens that bring the prophet bread and meat. It's a scene repeated in the lives of many early Christian saints and mystics who are so attuned to nature that the wild creatures are their helpers and not their predators.

When even the wadi dries up, Elijah is saved by the generosity of a widow and her son, who give the prophet the very last of their own provisions. But the jars of oil and food do not run dry in the whole time that Elijah stays with them. Whether this is due to a genuine miracle or the fact that the prophet stays with them and helps provide for all of them is up to your own interpretation. It is certainly a blessing of generosity.

After saving the life of the widow's son, the prophet Elijah returns to the Holy Land to confront King Ahab and Queen Jezebel and their prophets of Ba'al. Elijah issues a challenge to the prophets to see once and for all which god is mightier. The nation assembles on Mount Carmel to watch the prophets in their heavenly battle. Each side sacrifices a bull and places it on an altar. The prophets of Ba'al go first, but their sacrifice is to no avail, even though they pray themselves into a self-mutilating frenzy. When it's Elijah's turn, the prophet orders that the wood atop his stone altar be soaked with enough water that a pool forms in a trench around the altar. This handicap does not stop God, who sends down fire and burns the wet wood, the animal flesh, and even the stone altar. God is shown to be the master of the very elements themselves, and the people, convinced by the greatness of God, zealously return to the covenant.

Because of his victory over the prophets of Ba'al and winning of the people back to the covenant, Elijah must flee the wrath and death threats of King Ahab and Queen Jezebel (who have already murdered all of Elijah's fellow prophets of the Lord). Elijah is so distraught over this sudden turnaround after his apparent win on Mount Carmel that he prays for death. But God sends an angel with food and water. Elijah is ordered to rest, eat, and drink. Eventually, the prophet recovers and is sent to travel forty days and forty nights farther into the wilderness and to the top of Mount Horeb.

Elijah rests in a cave on one of the ancient high points while he waits for God to visit him. First, a mighty wind sweeps across the mountaintop, crushing rocks. But God is not in the wind. Next, an earthquake shakes the holy mountain. But God is not in the earthquake. Then, a fire rages over the mountain. But God is not in the fire.

It is ironic that God is in none of the events that we now refer to as acts of God. As I warned earlier, sometimes (most times) natural disasters are just that. We can bemoan their existence, mourn the destruction they cause, and work to prevent or lessen their future impact. But trying to read spiritual lessons into each one is folly, in part because it can cause us to miss the small things.

Elijah, after all these huge mountain-shaking events, is quiet enough to hear a tiny whispering sound. It was a sound that would have been so easy to miss; he could have been making too much noise to hear it or been too expectant of something even larger to pay attention to it. Fortunately, Elijah has the wisdom to remain patient and still, so he is present to the moment when it comes. And God's presence is so strong in this tiniest of sounds that the prophet covers his face and runs back into the cave to hide. That is when God asks Elijah—asks all of us—"Why are you here?" God is here, present in the elements, as revelation.

Even though King Solomon had built the Temple in the holy city of Jerusalem and made it the permanent home of the Ark of the Covenant, this story demonstrates that God is not confined to a sacred building. In fact, when the human-made sacred space is corrupted, God can still be found in the old places: the wilderness and the high points.

Meditation: Listening to the Elements

Water, wind, earth, and fire are the elemental energies of all creation. Imagine for a moment the earthiness of your body, its flesh that will one day return to the earth. Breathe in deeply and feel the invigoration of breath, air moving through your lungs. Put your hand on your pulse and feel the life-giving rhythm and flow of blood in your body made up mostly of water. Notice the heat your body produces, and become aware of the fire burning in you in those moments when you feel most alive.

What would it mean to listen into the deep wisdom of these four elements for our own spiritual direction and guidance in life as well as for wisdom about how to be present to others? Nature offers us this universal language with which to understand our own inner movements.

A reflection on each element below includes some questions and a simple practice you can engage in yourself, or you might bring it to your work with others as a way of calling upon that particular energetic quality.

Begin by centering yourself through the breath. Draw your breath deeply and slowly in and out. Imagine your awareness coming to rest in your heart center. This is a time of prayer and not a time of figuring things out. Open your heart to receive what gifts may come.

The Element of Air

All praise be Yours, my God, through Brothers Wind and Air,
And fair and stormy, all the weather's moods,
By which You cherish all that You have made.
 —St. Francis of Assisi, *Canticle of Creation*

You ride on the wings of the wind,
you make the winds your messengers
 —Psalm 104:3-4

St. Hildegard of Bingen saw the call of humanity as living in harmony and rhythm with the elements. In her worldview, the element of air is connected to the direction of the east and the rising sun. Air invites us to tend to our own journey of awakening and new life as we draw in each breath, welcoming this gift of life. This element is also connected to the energy of spring blossoming and the waxing of the moon.

Begin by facing the direction of the east, the direction of dawn and new beginnings, the hour when new life is breathed into us upon awakening. Imagine your own breath linking you to the breath of all living creatures. See the dance of breath: with each exhale, the plants take in the carbon dioxide and release oxygen; inhale and receive that gift offered.

- Where are you experiencing your own awakening?
- In what ways do you long to expand like your deep and spacious in-breath?
- As Mary Oliver asks, "Are you breathing just a little and calling it a life?"[7]

Hold these questions gently and listen for a response. Bow toward the east.

The Element of Fire

All praise be Yours, my God, through Brother Fire,
Through whom You brighten up the night.
How beautiful he is, how gay!
Full of power and strength.
    —St. Francis of Assisi, *Canticle of Creation*

I am the light of the world. Whoever follows me will never
walk in darkness but will have the light of life.
    —John 8:12

Hildegard connected the element of fire to the direction of the south and the heat of the noonday sun. Fire invites us to tend to our own journey of claiming the height of our passions and the desires that burn brightly in our hearts. This element is also connected to the energy of summer's ripeness and the full moon.

Turn and face the direction of the south, the hour of fullness and fire. Reconnect with your heart, the place of ignited passion and what St. John of the Cross calls "the living flame of love."[8] Bring compassion to yourself, to your loved ones, to your community, and to the world.

- Where is your passion? What sustains your inner fire?
- What are you invited to say yes to?
- In what ways do you long to burn more brightly?

Hold these questions gently and listen for a response. Bow toward the south.

The Element of Water

All praise be Yours, my God, through Sister Water,
So useful, humble, precious, and pure.
        —St. Francis of Assisi, *Canticle of Creation*

Let anyone who is thirsty come to me, and let the one who
believes in me drink. As the scripture has said: "Out of the
believer's heart shall flow rivers of living water."
        —John 7:38

Hildegard connects the element of water to the direction of the west and the setting sun. Water invites us to release into life's flow rather than forcing our own will upon life. This element is also connected to autumn's surrender and the waning moon.

Turn and face the direction of the west, the hour of waning light and endings, the time when we realize that time is limited. Water invites us to yield to the flow of our lives, to let our lives be organic.

* Where are you experiencing your own call to release and surrender?
* In what ways do you long to let go?
* Where is the flow of your life calling you to go?

Hold these questions gently and listen for a response. Bow toward the west.

The Element of Earth

All praise be Yours, my God, through Sister Earth, our mother,
Who feeds us in her sovereignty and produces
Various fruits and colored flowers and herbs.
        —St. Francis of Assisi, *Canticle of Creation*

I am the vine, you are the branches.

—John 15:5

Hildegard connects the element of earth to the direction of the north and the hour of midnight. Earth invites us to move into unknowing, darkness, and rest. This element is connected to winter's time of hibernation and the new moon.

Turn and face the direction of the north, the hour of darkness and mystery, the time of contemplation and letting go of our need to understand everything, with the invitation to rest fully. The earth and midnight also remind us of the reality of death. St. Benedict wrote in his Rule to "Day by day remind yourself that you are going to die."[9] This practice is to remind us to remember we are of the earth and will return there and to cherish each moment.

- How will you live knowing that you will one day return to the earth?
- Where are you called to more rest and spaciousness?
- What are you invited to say no to?

Hold these questions gently and listen for a response. Bow toward the north.

After completing this meditation, return your awareness to your own sacred center and rest in the presence of these wisdom guides. Offer gratitude for the gifts of wind, fire, water, and earth as spiritual directors for your journey. Spend a few minutes with your journal, making note of which elements called to you the most and which ones you felt the most resistance to.

Contemplative Walk: Elements as Witness

To witness means to be present to another in their experience without trying to change anything. The simple act of presence can be a balm and can allow things to shift and transform. This is the heart of spiritual direction and soul friendship: to act as a loving witness for another. Just having one's story heard and received is a transformative act. Nature offers us this loving presence.

Begin your contemplative walk in the usual way by centering your-self with some deep breaths and bringing your awareness from your head down to your heart. Set your intention for this time to be as fully present as you can be, and listen for how nature wants to meet you wherever you are.

As you walk, bring your concerns of the heart to Earth and the el-ements. You don't have to seek transformation; instead, simply allow yourself to be seen, heard, witnessed, and held in whatever you are ex-periencing. Offer whatever is weighing on your heart or sparking your passions and dreams. Give this to the wind, to the water, to the earth, and to the fire. Listen for the wisdom being offered in return. Then offer grat-itude for being received in this way.

When you return home, spend some time journaling about what you noticed and discovered.

Herbal Invitation: Sacred Smoke and Incense

Incense is one of the forms of herbal practice still regularly used in many churches, especially the high church traditions such as Catholicism or Episcopalianism. In the story of the magi visiting the infant Jesus on Epiphany, they bring him gifts of gold, frankincense, and myrrh. Those last two are often used for burning in sacred settings.

We can make use of incense in our homes as well to clear the air, to bless, and to bring a sacred intention to prayer. There are two ways to burn plant material for sacred use. The first is as incense. For this you will need a charcoal disk and an incense bowl. Look for incense charcoal, as it is usually fast lighting. Use a match or lighter to ignite the charcoal, place it in the incense holder or bowl, and then sprinkle some incense or plant resin and dried leaves on top of the disk. You can purchase myrrh resin and feel a connection to those ancient magi, or you can take any dried herb and add some to burn. Let the smoke guide your prayers to commu-nion with the Divine Presence. Since early times, this act of letting the smoke rise like prayer has been an integral part of ritual. The psalmist says, "Let my prayer be counted as incense before you" (Ps 141:2).

The other way to burn plant materials is as sacred smoke sticks, which means to take a bundle of dried herbs tied together and light the tip so that smoke is released. I often bundle small bunches of rosemary, let them dry, and then use them for purification of a space. Rosemary is quite easy to grow. I sometimes add mugwort and sage to the bundle as well. Sacred smoke can be used for an altar or to help clear away any unwanted energies, but it also invokes a sense of blessing. In churches, you sometimes see priests using a censer to bless the altar and holy book. People often burn incense in their homes when they have gone through a transition. You can also bless yourself or another person with sacred smoke by offering a prayer of something that needs to be released and then circling the smoke around the person being blessed.

You might choose to grow particular herbs in your garden specifically for incense and sacred smoke. When you plant them, offer blessings and prayers of gratitude for their growth and eventual service to you. Receive the plants as gift when you harvest, and ask that they help support you and clear whatever is not needed.

Visual Art Exploration: Create an Altar of the Elements

Consider creating an altar at home with symbols of the four elements present as a reminder of the soul wisdom they offer to you.

In the direction of the east place a feather or some incense on your altar in honor of wind and air.

In the direction of the south place a candle on your altar in honor of fire.

In the direction of the west place a bowl of water or a shell on your altar in honor of water. Consider going to a nearby body of water—a river, lake, or ocean—and scooping up the water to place in your bowl. Change this regularly to keep the water fresh.

In the direction of the north place a stone, dried leaves, or other natural objects on your altar in honor of earth.

In the center you might place a cross to help anchor everything in a central symbol and as a reminder of how everything in each direction is sacred.

Spend some time each day with your altar just noticing where your energy and attention are drawn. Ask that element what wisdom it might have to offer to you that day. Offer a prayer to the God of creation, who gifts us the elements as guides, to support you through their wisdom.

Written Exploration: "I Am" Poem

You might begin by doing an online search for a poem by N. Scott Momaday titled "The Delight Song of Tsoai-Talee." Then read some of the participant poems below that were inspired by this work.

Drawing on the poems as a springboard, write your own version of an "I am" poem. Let images arise spontaneously without editing, always returning to the words "I am" and listening for what parts of creation you are longing to identify with. Imagine speaking from the voice of creation, and see what wants to be spoken. As you deepen your own capacity to cherish Earth and feel your intimacy with her being, what do you notice and discover?

Previous Participant Poems

Crow cries
I hear and tilt my head.
See the world.
Tilt and shift
See differently.
Delighted by bright, shiny things

Rock rests
Solid under me.
Cold, hard, holding in.
Teased warm by the sun
Opens slowly,
Stories told.

River rolls
Drawing me
I float, flow
Swirl in eddies,
Tumble over rocks.
A journey of adventure.

Flowers unfurl.
Petals—pink, white, yellow.
Visual spring after
Invisible winter.
Learn patience.
Beauty awaits.

—Evelyn Jackson

I am star singing with the wind
I am frog grunting at the shoreline
I am tall tree living boundaries.
I am chickadee fluttering a seed.
I am mist holding up the rainbow
I am lake, reflecting sky.
I am love, embracing my beloved.
I am mother, made of joy and grief.
I am starchy snowflake disappeared.
I am stolen sun nourishing blooms.
I am gale flying in forest
I am soft-soaking rain.
I am stranger, smiling high.

—Margo Nagle

I am the eye of the hawk, scanning.
I am the beak of the raven, tearing.
I am iron pyrite, glistening.

I am black clouds and wind
and the soft green needles

of the redwood growing damp.
I am the paws of a dog on snow
and the yellow crystals left behind.
I am thistles caught in wool
and thistledown floating on the wind.
I am the moon.

—Kake Huck

I am the wind's breath
I am the flame's shadow
I am the water's reflection
I am the sun's kiss

I am the moonlight's embrace
I am the raindrop's edge
I am my mother's child,
I am hope incarnate.

—Jeannette Beeger

I am the Stone calling out "Draw me."
I am the Golden Leaf, dying to whom I have been. I am the White
　　Dog, letting one thing lead to another. I am the Vulture with
　　wings spread, moving with the Moving.
I am the Sun, radiating warmth and generosity to all. I am the
　　Geminid meteor shower, greeting the long dark of the night. I
　　am the Moon, walking together with Mars in the evening sky.
I am the Raindrop, embarking on a journey of which it knows not
　　the final destination.
I am the Journey, holding the arrow and letting the arrow steer me.

—Dolores Nice-Siegenthaler

I am white pine
sculpted by wind.
I am pink granite,
smoothed by water.
I am orange path of the moon
crossing the lake.
I am big dipper,
pointing home.
I am river current
carrying everything away.
I am hemlock grove,
hosting wild turkeys.
I am loon
calling for its mate.
I am Antares,
ancient star fading.
I am grey beech
holding golden leaves through winter.
I am red fox
curiously watching.
I am snowshoe hare
changing colour in season.
I am veins of quartz
striping Georgian Bay granite.
I am all that lives in me:
as memory, as wonder, as gift.

—Anne Beattie-Stokes

Closing Blessing

In this chapter we considered Earth and her elements as the original spiritual directors. You were invited to open yourself to the wise guidance offered to you by creatures; by water, wind, earth, and fire; and by time spent in nature. We might remember that we are not alone, that these elements companion us as they reveal the Divine Presence and give direction to us.

A Morning Blessing (Inspired by Mercedes Sosa)

Gracias a la vida, que me ha dado tanto. Ceniza, tierra, lodo,
    piedra, arena, polvo.
Compost dirt, mud, stone, sand, dust

Gracias a l vida. El verde del límon, hoja obscura, la Yerba, el
    umbral de la falda del sauce que da le sombra.
Light leaves dark leaves, lawn, the skirt of the willow who offers
    shade.

Que me ha dado tanto. Las flores del verano- la rosa, geranium,
    la margarita, que toman y chupan los gotes de la lluvia.
Summer flowers—rose, geranium, daisy that drink and gulp down
    rainwater.

Gracias a la vida. El himno de los pajaritos, los animales peluch-
    es, gusanos, pinches, las moscas, y la abeja y que da nos luz
    por miel.
Birdsong, furry ones, worms, midge, flies and the bee's life giving
    honey.

Gracias a la vida. El sol, el mar, la luna el corriente de las horas,
    y todos Uds. Polvo de las estrellas. Que me ha dado tanto,
the current of the hours and to you, all stardust,

que me ha dado tanto.
which has given me so much.

                           –Jillian Ross

CHAPTER 5

EARTH AS THE ORIGINAL ICON

QUESTION: And what is the fruit of study?
ANSWER: To perceive the eternal Word of God
reflected in every plant and insect, every bird and animal, and
every man and woman.

—St. Ninian[1]

Icons play a significant role in the Eastern Orthodox Christian tradition. Theologically, icons are considered to be sacred as they offer a doorway to communion between heaven and Earth. Icon writing is rooted in the theology of the Incarnation, with Christ being the icon of God, and the icon forms a visible gospel. Often part of the practice is to kiss the icon to show love and devotion toward Christ.

Nature is a holy text for many of us, and an icon is a window to the Divine Presence at work in the world. Creation is therefore the original icon, the primordial place of our encounter with God, the Great Artist, who is continually at work in the world around us.

St. Hildegard of Bingen saw the presence of the Holy through what she called *viriditas*, which essentially means the greening power of God. This greening operates on the physical level and is how plants and trees flourish by gathering energy within them for full growth. But it also operates on the spiritual level. Our souls can be greening, or they might feel as if they are arid and dry. For Hildegard, this was a sign that the Divine was at work, when the greening power was able to flow freely through

creatures, plants, and human souls. Looking at how the body was flourishing and how it might reflect the inner state of being was her unique
principle of discernment.

This outward greening was an icon for Hildegard, a visible image of
the presence of the Spirit at work. We do not need other than what is already here. Creation has revealed the face of the Divine in our midst if we
only have eyes to see. When we open ourselves to the greening present all
around us, we see the Divine already at work in nature.

Angela of Foligno was a thirteenth-century Franciscan mystic. She
saw the presence of the Holy in the world in a different way, writing,

> Immediately, the eyes of my soul were opened, and in a vision
> I saw God's wholeness and the wholeness of creation. In the
> sea, and also in everything beyond the sea in outer space, I saw
> nothing but God's power and God's presence. It was totally in-
> describable. My soul was overcome with wonder at everything.
> I shouted, "The world is pregnant with God!" That's when I
> understood how small creation is when the enormity of God is
> considered. God's power fills the sea and everything beyond it.[2]

This sense of the world being pregnant with the Divine Presence is the
heart of the Incarnation and also the doorway into an icon. The icon reveals this fullness, allowing us to open our eyes and suddenly see things
with a sense of wonder. By paying close attention to nature as a window
into the divine nature, we learn how God works in our lives.

The Franciscan monk St. Bonaventure offers us another image for the
way that nature can reveal itself to be an icon: "Just as you see that a ray
of light entering through a window is colored in different ways according
to the different colors of the various parts, so the divine ray shines forth
in each and every creature in different ways and in different properties."[3]
God's light pours through every created thing, each in unique ways, so
that the whole diversity and spectrum of the Sacred is shown to us.

Making Space for the Grief

One of the things we can see clearly through prayerful vision is the havoc humanity has unleashed on nature. Nature as icon reveals to us both the glory of divine creation and also the reality of human development and the rampant use of plastics, toxins, chemicals, and fossil fuels.

An essential part of the contemplative path toward deepened intimacy with nature is to see the truth of things and to discern what we are being called to release in terms of habits, practices, and ways of being that burden us and weigh us down as well as those habits that bring harm to Earth.

We all know that we need to live more lightly, consume less, and produce less waste for Earth to thrive. What are the attitudes or beliefs that we can also release to make more space for something new? Perhaps it is a feeling of overwhelm or hopelessness when we think about our impact on Earth. Small actions do add up, shifting our thought patterns to a way of hope; moving forward is essential.

Also essential is the act of lament. Lament releases the layers of grief we are holding and makes room within us for the Spirit to break through in new ways. We live in a culture that denies pain and suffering and encourages every possible method of distraction or cheering ourselves up. We deny the reality of disorientation and grief as we live surrounded by messages of "be strong," "move on," or "think positive."

Theologian Walter Brueggemann writes powerfully about the biblical tradition of lament and the profound necessity of lamenting for our health as human beings.[4] A full one-third of the book of Psalms is psalms of lament. Brueggemann calls them the psalms of disorientation that lift up attention to the pain of human loss without assigning judgment to them. The reality of pain is a given. When we deny this pain, we become prone to guilt and to becoming trapped in the spiral of self-blame and paralysis. These psalms offer us as individuals and as communities of faith a way to pray together, speaking truth about pain and naming the reality we live in.

Our churches generally do not offer us resources on how to grieve well. Often traditional language relies heavily on the hope-and-resurrection side of things, forgetting the death, suffering, and descent parts of the story. Brueggmann describes lament as a necessary act of truth-telling.

Acknowledging that something is not right loosens the cry stuck in our throats and softens the hardness of our hearts. We must journey through the experience of abandonment and death to reach resurrection. There is no way out, only through.

Collectively we have denied so much grief for so long that for many of us it feels frightening to even consider allowing ourselves to sink into the sorrow our bodies hold. Both personal sorrow over all the ways we have been wounded and collective sorrow over all the injustices enacted in the name of our species—our bodies hold this pain, and when it is not expressed, it becomes frozen within us.

Author and environmental activist Joanna Macy describes the power in letting ourselves experience our collective pain over Earth.[5] When we hold back, we become incapable of acting in meaningful ways. When we repress pain, Macy says we tend toward three main coping strategies—disbelief, denial, and double life. We have difficulty taking in the reality of what is happening to Earth, so we don't let ourselves fully grasp its magnitude. We continue to live in the same ways, maintaining a kind of superficial cheerfulness to get through the day.

To behold Earth as an icon of Sacred Presence, we must also wrestle with how Earth reveals the terrible things we have unleashed upon her. Lament is a necessary first step toward healing. We are in the midst of what St. John of the Cross might call a "dark night" experience collectively, one in which we are standing at an impasse. Theologian Constance Fitzgerald describes what *impasse* means:

> By impasse, I mean that there is no way out of, no way around, no rational escape from, what imprisons one, no possibilities in the situation. In a true impasse, every normal manner of acting is brought to a standstill, and ironically, impasse is experienced not only in the problem itself but also in any solution rationally attempted. Every logical solution remains unsatisfying, at the very least. The whole life situation suffers a depletion, has the word limits written upon it. . . . Any movement out, any next step, is canceled, and the most dangerous temptation is to give up, to quit, to surrender to cynicism and despair, in the face of

the disappointment, disenchantment, hopelessness, and loss of meaning that encompass one.[6]

We know many of the next steps we need to take as a society and as a world to deal with the issues we are facing. However, as individuals, we often feel completely helpless at the denial or inaction of our elected leaders.

In a genuine experience of impasse, our usual ways of operating become frozen. Our left-brained analytical approach to life—where we try to force solutions and reason things out—is ineffective, and so the right brain becomes activated, bringing its gifts of intuition and creativity and suggesting solutions outside of our perceived expectations. Fitzgerald describes this as a "reverse pressure on the imagination," in which the imagination is the only way forward.

It must be stressed, writes theologian Dorothee Soelle, that if the suffering of the impasse is not allowed expression, "there is a corresponding disappearance of passion for life and of the strength and intensity of its joys."[7] Finding ourselves in this state of impasse, we must discover ways of expressing the deep pain and anguish we feel, or we will be destroyed by it or made completely numb by apathy. Lament is a necessary stage in the creative resolution of terrible situations and suffering. This opens the new pathway through and ahead.

The experiences of mystics across time reassure us that the usual rational ways of proceeding are of no use, but when we allow ourselves to have the experience of impasse—when we move fully into it and allow our hearts to experience grief—then transformation can enter in.

The Practice of Lament

We are called to name the sorrow and suffering we experience on behalf of Earth. In expressing it we avoid our sorrow becoming dysfunctional. Repressed pain gets projected onto the world around us and either causes more suffering or reinforces the sense of inaction many of us hold. When we create room for the pain to move through us, we create conditions for catharsis. However, this is not to imply that by simply expressing our grief over Earth, we somehow move through it. But by expressing our grief we can discover a kinship of grief with one another and feel a deeper solidarity with all of Earth's creatures. We experience pain over Earth's creatures because of our interconnection with them. When we remember that we arise from Earth, we recognize that the lament of Earth moves through our bodies and hearts as well.

When we discover that we don't need to be afraid of our pain, that we can stand witness and bear it, we release a tremendous amount of energy for living. We may realize that the anguish we experience is verification that we are indeed radically connected to Earth. Our capacity to grieve is evidence of our ability to enter into compassion.

Endurance of Stone

Perhaps one of the most unexpected gifts of living in Ireland has been falling in love with stone. I always loved collecting stones on beaches and along rivers before, but I never gave much thought to the type of rock I was collecting.

Living in Galway, we are on the meeting point of two very different geological landscapes. To the south is the Burren, a limestone landscape of huge significance because it is one of the few karst landscapes in the world, meaning the bedrock is exposed. It is also unique botanically in that flowers from alpine, arctic, and Mediterranean climates grow alongside one another there. People travel from all over the world to study and view this spectacle, especially in spring and summer when the wildflowers blossom in profusion.

Because of the exposed limestone, there is a strange quality to the landscape there. Limestone is soft and porous, so the stone is often worn smooth with many holes through it, and the water goes underground. When you walk there, it often looks as though you are walking across the moon. The Burren is also the place with the highest density of ecclesiastical sites in all of Ireland, likely because the ancient monks sought a wilderness place, much like the desert mothers and fathers before them in Syria and Egypt.

To the west of us is the region known as Connemara, which is made of granite and some marble and quartz. These are hard stones, jagged and angular. The mountains have peaks reaching up to the sky, and the water stays above ground and collects in the many beautiful lakes there. Connemara is also covered with bog. A lot of sheep graze there because they can find sustenance on land with short growth. Heather and gorse grow in abundance.

The stones speak to me of the endurance of things and how nature will persist. When I spend time among granite and limestone, I remember all of the prayers uttered by the generations of people living in these sacred landscapes. I find myself aware of being part of a great lineage of people trying to live well and find meaning.

The stones are an icon of grace; they reveal to me a face of the Divine that endures and is ever-patient with the world's unfolding. The endless burdens we carry and the stories we tell ourselves that pull us away from the divine creatures we have been created to be are what get us in our own way. The next time you are among stones or trees, see if you might imagine laying your heavy burdens down and letting the mountains or seas carry them.

St. Columba and His Horse

St. Columba (or St. Columcille as he is known in Ireland) is probably most famous for setting off across the Irish Sea in a small boat to found the abbey on the island of Iona in Scotland, which is still an active community today.

One of the stories about him is that he had a much-loved horse. On the day that St. Columba was going to die, his horse approached him, knowing he was about to lose his dear friend. The horse began to weep.

I love this story of Columba's animal companion expressing his grief so freely. There is much research to indicate the rich emotional lives that animals have and how they experience connection and loss, joy and sadness. This story for me is an icon of the tenderness of God.

---◈---

Scripture Reflection
from John Valters Paintner

Working Together for Freedom (Romans 8:19–23)

> For the creation waits with eager longing for the revealing
> of the children of God; for the creation was subjected to futility,
> not of its own will but by the will of the one who subjected it,
> in hope that the creation itself will be set free from its bondage
> to decay and will obtain the freedom of the glory of the chil-
> dren of God. We know that the whole creation has been groan-
> ing in labor pains until now; and not only the creation, but we
> ourselves, who have the first fruits of the Spirit, groan inwardly
> while we wait for adoption, the redemption of our bodies.

> −Romans 8:19-23

St. Paul's letter to the community in Rome is not unlike his other epistles.
He begins with a flowery yet humble opening before addressing specific
issues of the emerging church, and so gives universal advice for the faithful throughout the centuries.

This new Christian church in Rome has numerous, diverse members.
They are Jews and Gentiles who have come to follow the way of Jesus.
But as any Christian can attest, following Jesus is no guarantee of an
untroubled life or harmonious community. We all (both personally and
collectively) have issues and oftentimes problems. Humans are complex
creatures. And while society offers many benefits to make life easier,
there are many trade-offs. We don't always get along with one another,
and we all need a little help from time to time. St. Paul writes to offer
encouragement and guidance when needed.

In the first part of his epistle, Paul discusses idolatry, justification by faith, and the difference between living life according to the Law and living life according to the Spirit. This last one had become a point of contention between the Jewish Christians and the Gentile Christians.

Those in the church of Rome with Jewish heritage are, understandably, focused on the Law of Moses. It is how they were raised and what they know. For them, Jesus Christ is the fulfillment of the long-awaited Messiah. But the Gentiles in the community were drawn to the Church by the Spirit of Jesus, and so the Law is of secondary importance. In Romans 8, Paul is attempting to bring the community together by focusing on what they have in common: freedom in Christ.

It's a central theme to Christianity, one at the core of Church doctrine. But what is unique here is that Paul is placing an urgency on this liberation. He states that all creation is groaning in anticipation of the fruits of the Spirit, that all creation is waiting for humanity to be fully birthed into our true selves.

The different backgrounds of the members of the church in Rome, according to St. Paul, are trivial in comparison to the shared destiny that lies before us all. And so, just as all creation works together to bring forth the fruits of spring, so too should the Church community work together to bring forth the fruits of the Spirit. Just as all creation rejoices at the first fruits, so too should we all rejoice in the blessings of one another.

Nature is very diverse. It is not just in the myriad of species on Earth that we find diversity but also in the elements. It is the inanimate minerals in the soil and the water that feeds the seed for it to sprout and grow. It is the bees that pollinate the plants and the wind and wild animals that scatter the seeds. All these things and more work in harmony to bring forth life. And it only takes the disruption of one component to throw off the balance of the whole. We can hear Earth groaning in response.

Whether it is soil erosion due to overfarming, water pollution due to industrial runoff, killing of insects due to pesticides, the extinction of animal species due to human encroachment, or climate change due to fossil fuel use, when we interfere with the balance of nature, we all suffer. This loss needs to be acknowledged and mourned before we can heal. When we make time to gaze upon nature and take a long, loving look at the consequences of our actions, our first step must be to groan in lament alongside creation, for we are part of creation as well.

Meditation: An Ecological Examen

St. Ignatius of Loyola, a fifteenth-century Spanish mystic and the founder of the Jesuits, suggested the daily practice of the Examen, which essentially is to ask yourself two questions at the end of each day: What has been most life-giving? What has been most life-draining? I invite you into an adaptation of this practice that invites a deeper ecological awareness. Consider praying with these questions over a period of a few days, and notice what patterns arise.

Center yourself, move inward, breathe deeply, and enter the stillness of your heart.

In your imagination, reflect on this last day, perhaps the last twenty-four-hour period (although you could do this prayer each week and reflect on several days). As you move through the memories of your experiences, reflect: When have you been most deeply aware of the beauty of creation? When have you experienced yourself as a participant in nature rather than an observer? When did you hold an Earth-cherishing consciousness? Where was nature revealed as an icon of the Divine? When did you experience the fullness of greening in your own being?

Notice which experiences arise, and let one be your focus for prayer. Savor this moment, breathe it in, let it have room to expand, and become aware of how it feels in your body. Offer gratitude for this experience, and then let it go.

Return to your imagination and walk through this last day again. When have you been most disconnected from nature? When were you most distracted? When did you rush through life? When were you unaware or unconscious? Was there a moment when you felt wasteful or exploiting of Earth's resources? When did creation as icon feel like a distant awareness? Were there moments when your own soul felt arid and dry?

Again, notice which moment rises up for you. Let one experience be the focus for your prayer. Breathe it in as well, and notice how it feels in your body. Try not to resist it, but let it have room in you to be held with compassion and gentleness. See if you might offer forgiveness to yourself for this moment.

Breathe deeply again and let this go.

Reflect for a few moments on what grace you most need to support you through this next day.

Gently bring your awareness back to the room.

It can be very helpful to journal and write down these moments from your life, so that over time you can begin to see the patterns.

Contemplative Walk: Earth as Companion in Grief

> I will be like the dew to Israel;
> > he shall blossom like the lily,
> > he shall strike root like the forests of Lebanon
>
> His shoots shall spread out;
> > his beauty shall be like the olive tree,
> > and his fragrance like that of Lebanon.
>
> They shall again live beneath my shadow,
> > they shall flourish as a garden;
>
> they shall blossom like the vine,
> > their fragrance shall be like the wine of Lebanon.
>
> —Hosea 14:5-7

Begin your contemplative walk in the usual way by centering yourself with some deep breaths and bringing your awareness from your head down to your heart. Set an intention for this time to be as fully present as you can, and listen for how nature wants to speak to you.

As you walk, bring your concerns of the heart to Earth. Allow yourself to feel grief and anger, sadness and overwhelm at what is happening to nature at human hands. Let the tears flow. Notice if some aspect of nature is inviting you closer, whether a tree, stone, leaf, or another element. Let this part of nature be present to whatever you are feeling; give your feelings over to Earth as an offering; feel yourself as not alone in this grief and pain.

In this walk, allow nature to be your witness by its presence to you, which can transform. You don't have to seek this transformation, but simply allow yourself to be seen, to be heard, to be witnessed, and to be held in whatever you are experiencing. Then offer gratitude for being received in this way.

Nature has a way of offering us consolation. I know that was my experience after my mother died and my daily walks among autumn and winter trees sustained me in a way nothing else could. The passage from Hosea above speaks to me of the consolation that nature can offer to our hearts. The dew, the blossoms, the shoots spreading, and the beauty and fragrance all speak to how God engages natural elements to reveal God's heart to us.

When you return home, spend some time journaling about what you noticed and discovered.

Herbal Invitation: Rose Anointing Oil

Rose is perhaps one of my favorite herbs to work with, not the least of which because it was also a favorite of St. Hildegard of Bingen. In her book on plant properties she describes rose as a healer of the heart and as an herb that augments or amplifies all the other herbs in a medicine. Because of its properties, she tended to include it in almost everything she created, writing, "Rose is also good to add to potions, unguents, and all medications. If even a little rose is added, they are so much better, because of the good virtues of the rose."[8]

Roses have, of course, a magnificent scent and are often celebrated for their beauty. I love the gorgeous petals and the thorns, a reminder that boundaries are a healthy thing. Roses are also associated with the Virgin Mary; many apparitions of her have included roses, such as Our Lady of Guadalupe, and one of the names for Mary is "Mystical Rose."

I am going to suggest two ways of working with rose to create an anointing oil. For the first possibility, a rose-infused oil, you will want to use dried organic petals. You can use fresh rose petals if you have access to them—just be sure they haven't been sprayed, and allow them to dry for twenty-four to forty-eight hours in a cool, dark place before placing them in the oil.

Please note that herb-infused oils are different than essential oils. Making essential oils requires loads more plant material and more sophisticated technology than making herb-infused oils. Herb-infused oils are simple to make and have a much more gentle scent than that of essential oil, while still carrying medicinal properties.

For the first way of creating an anointing oil, begin by centering yourself and offering a blessing for this time of sacred work with the herb and plant allies. You will be creating an oil for anointing yourself, so bless this time with whatever qualities you would like to be anointed with later. Spend time just being with the rose petals and their scent and texture.

Take a small, clean glass jar, and fill it three-quarters full with dried rose petals. If you wish, you can gently break up the petals with your fingers first (making sure hands are clean), or you can use a mortar and pestle.

Fill the jar to the top with a carrier oil of your choice. You could use extra virgin olive oil, sweet almond oil, jojoba oil, or another oil that is suitable for the skin.

Put the lid on the jar and shake it to distribute the oil through the herbs. Place a label on the jar with the materials used and the date. Then place the jar in a cool, dark place such as a cupboard, and shake it daily. Each time you shake the jar, offer blessings for your creation and ponder the unfolding of your life right now.

After four weeks, or a full moon cycle, strain the oil into a clean bowl. You can use some cheesecloth or muslin to strain and then squeeze any excess oil from the rose petals.

The strained liquid is your finished oil. The scent of roses is likely to be very light. You can add essential oils at this time if there are any additional scents you would like to include.

The second (and much quicker) method for creating an anointing oil is simply to add essential oil of rose (usually as a dilution called either rose absolute or rose otto as pure rose oil is very expensive) to a carrier oil that is good for the skin. You can say a prayer and blessing as you add a few drops of the rose oil to the carrier, shake it up, and receive the gift.

Make some time for anointing yourself. This might become a daily practice. Because rose is especially effective for the heart, you might consider blessing your heart with the oil and asking for healing in whatever area of life you need right now. Rose can help to hold us in our grief over Earth and meet us in that place of lament. You can ask that the Spirit work through these physical objects for greater healing and vibrancy.

Bless your intentions with the oil, perhaps marking your forehead, your lips, your throat, your hands, or another part of your body that needs extra attention. Say a blessing for each part as you anoint with the oil. Anointing is an ancient practice and is still offered at baptism as well as to those who are ill.

Visual Art Exploration: Writing or Painting on Stones

Go on a contemplative walk this week to let a stone find you. This is different than going out to look for the perfect stone. Try instead to let yourself be discovered. Open yourself to receive the gift of a stone (or more than one as the case may be). Or you may already have a special stone at home that you want to work with.

When you return home with your special stone, consider writing a word or phrase on it to serve as a reminder or a talisman. Fine-point Sharpie pens work very well for this, but any marker will do. Is there a way to remind yourself to be present to nature as holy icon each day? Is there a prayer for Earth's healing you might offer? Can you place your stone somewhere it will act as a visual reminder?

Written Exploration: Prayer of Lament

Make space to experience your grief. Create a space of time, maybe an hour once a week, to give yourself over to the pain and suffering of Earth.

This might feel awkward at first, but the limited time creates a safe container in which you can allow the expression to come through. Sometimes we don't give ourselves over to grief because we fear that we will not come back out. But when we do allow the pain to move through us, we find that it has its own rhythm of rising and subsiding.

Movement is a great way to access sorrow. Play a piece of music that has a slow quality of lament to it. Let your body move in whatever way it longs to. We store so much grief within our muscles and tissues that even gentle movement can unleash tears.

If writing is a helpful way for you to name and process your grief, you could also practice keeping a lament journal. This can be done by following the structure of a psalm of lament:

- **Address to God:** How do you call upon the Divine Presence—God?
- **Complaint:** What is your lament and cry of pain?
- **Affirmation of trust:** Have you had an experience of God meeting you in your pain before? Draw on this memory to experience a sense of companionship in your grief.
- **Petition:** What is your deepest desire from God? What do you want for Earth?
- **Assurance of being heard:** What do you need from God to feel witnessed?
- **Vow of praise:** What can you promise or offer to God on behalf of your longing?
- **Hymn or blessing:** Is there something for which you can express gratitude or wonder or delight?

Previous Participant Poems

Lament

O, great and ever-present Source
Ground of all being and life

How long must we wait for the mindless raging destruction of our
    earth to cease?
How long must the innocent suffer the cruelty and ignorance of
    the few?
How long must we grieve the destruction of life, of communities
    and civilizations?

I have known you in birdsong and bright berries in the bleakness
    of loss
Somehow I trust even as I doubt, as I question you and myself

O, how I long for our hearts to be opened in love, to love
For tenderness, forgiveness, and mercy to bless our days and each
    other

You are present in the compassion of those who care in the midst
    of devastated lives
I feel you in the wind, the rain, and the sunshine that caress my
    face to remind me

O, let us be the hope, carriers of your light for the world
In all we do and share with those we encounter in the dailyness
    of our lives
Let us bring your healing touch

May we create kind circles of belonging
May we dance your peace through our days
May we joyfully sing your praise

O, great and ever-present Source
Ground of all being and life
We thank you!

—Felicity Collins

Ah, Yahweh, creator of all being,
very breath of our breath
How can we bear this suffering
day after day after day?
Your willful lost children
trying to grab what they can
and write their own rules
over and over and over again!
Lashing out heedlessly
to take territory,
make a statement,
punish those who see things differently.
They kill innocent people.
They kill innocent animals.
They kill innocent plants.
They ruin the very lands
which they want to possess.
And we, your supposedly faithful children,
we do not stop it.
We do not speak out.
We do not see our complicity.
I know you felt human anguish on the Cross.
I know you suffer with us, within us,
I know your presence with us in every horror.
In the depths of my grief,
unable to relieve my beloved's suffering
You cradled me in your hands.
Hold the world now in those hands.
Break open our hearts to healing
And show us the path
to help you heal our beloved world.
You are the love, the beloved, and the loving.
You are all we need to be. Healed.

—Sharon Handy

O all present Source of Life, I weep for those many members of
the Earth Community . . . bird, fish, four-legged, human, etc.
who have lost their habitat and wander in search of a sustain-
able home, fearing extinction.

You animate all and remain ever present within each, grieving
with them and with me. Forgive my complicity in the causes
of Earth's suffering.

Help us all to find ways to work together to bring healing to our
beloved Earth.

—Nancy Audette

Closing Blessing

This chapter we have considered Earth as the original icon. Pause a little
while and simply breathe in the beauty of creation's presence. Imagine
the place in nature where you could experience yourself fully diving in
as with the sea or resting on the mossy ground of the forest or a warm
rock on a mountain. Notice which place comes to you as icon in this
moment, and simply rest into an imagined experience of letting yourself
come home fully.

Allow yourself also the space for lament or grief to rise up, knowing
that nature will meet you in this space, console you, and inspire you with
ways to move forward.

Blessed be the ants and worms who toil
Unseen and underground to bless our soil
Blessed be the frogs and water creatures
Tadpoles, toads, and newts and water beetles
Blessed be the plants that we call weeds
Because they do not meet our human needs
Blessed be the mice, the rats, the shrews,
The animals for which we have no use
Blessed be the birds who only caw
The raven, rook, and crow and the jackdaw
(Horseflies and bugs that bite and wasps that sting

I know I often call them blessed things)
Let's bless the midge and let it be forgiven
It has its place and purpose under heaven.

—Alix Brown

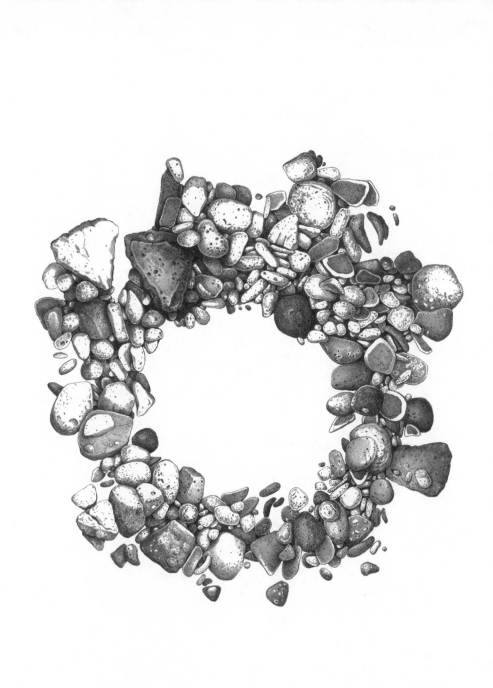

CHAPTER 6

EARTH AS THE ORIGINAL SACRAMENT

I once spoke to my friend, an old squirrel, about the Sacraments—
he got so excited

and ran into a hollow in his tree and came
back holding some acorns, an owl feather,
and a ribbon he had found.

And I just smiled and said, "Yes, dear,
you understand:
everything imparts
God's grace."

    —St. Francis of Assisi, "The Sacraments"[1]

One of the classic definitions of a sacrament is something that is an outward, visible sign of an inward, invisible grace. In the Christian church there are different rituals that are considered to be sacraments. The Catholic Church has seven sacraments, while other denominations count fewer among their number. However, this idea of sacramentality extends beyond the formal sacraments such as Baptism, Matrimony, Communion, and the Anointing of the Sick. This sense of sacramentality, rooted in the Incarnation, extends our vision out to the world so that everything can be a sacrament, meaning every person, creature, plant, and object can be an opportunity to encounter something of the Divine Presence in the world.

Sacramentality is a quality present in creation that opens us up to the Sacred Presence in all things. Sacraments reveal grace.

When viewed through this expansive lens, we discover that the more we cultivate intimacy with the natural world, the more we discover about God's presence. All of our interactions with nature can be sacramental, and all the ways nature extends herself to us are sacramental as well. Sacramentality breaks through our surface obsessions in the world and plunges us into the depth of the Sacred at every turn. It is a spontaneous reminder of God's creative upwelling and expansive love, calling us to love beyond boundaries. St. Isaac the Syrian defines a charitable heart as one "which is burning with love for the whole creation, for [humans], for the birds, for the beasts, for the demons—for all creatures."[2]

This discovery that every creature and every created thing can be a window of revelation into the divine nature is an invitation to fall more and more in love with the world. To see that teachers of grace exist everywhere means to bring a sense of reverence to the way we walk in the world. When we encounter nature as sacrament, we can no longer objectify it. We can instead create the circumstances that nurture and nourish this kind of vision.

The fourth-century mystic St. Basil has this prayer attributed to him:

> Enlarge within us the sense of
> fellowship with all living things,
> our brothers the animals to whom you
> gave the earth as their home in
> common with us.[3]

Sacramental vision means not only that we grow in our love of God's ways in the world but also that we grow in our sense of kinship with creation.

Holy Indifference

This sense of the sacramentality of all creation reveals to us the God of immanence—the One who is intimately involved in our world and who expresses divine love through the created world. However, there is also the transcendent dimension of God, in which we recognize God's wholly otherness. The sacraments of nature can also reveal this aspect of the Divine to us.

One of the things I find most refreshing about my own time in nature, whether in the woods, by the sea, or climbing a mountain, is nature's sense of holy indifference. Being among trees hundreds of years old or stones millions of years old, or walking along the primordial sea, my own problems become small and seem less significant. I am able to breathe more deeply and experience a freedom from my own narrow vision of the world. I remember a God who is vast and whose horizons extend far beyond my own limited knowing and imagination.

Religious scholar Andrew Harvey writes, "The things that ignore us save us in the end. Their presence awakens silence in us; they refresh our courage with the purity of their detachment."[4] I like to imagine this as another dimension of the trees as holy ones: they offer their witness of detachment, of ease and presence, reminding us that this moment now is what matters. One aspect of sacrament is an encounter with the awesomeness and transcendence of the Divine. We are given a sense of perspective on our lives and concerns.

Saints and Ravens

There are many stories of saints who have had encounters with ravens. St. Benedict is often depicted with a raven in icons of him. Stories tell us some fellow monks were trying to poison him through the bread he had to eat. One day the raven came and took it from his hands to save his life.

St. Anthony and St. Paul were both hermits in the desert, but they were also soul friends to one another. A raven would feed Paul a half loaf of bread each day, but when his companion was visiting, the raven brought them a whole loaf.

Elijah is also said to have been fed by ravens. God appointed them to bring him meat (see 1 Kgs 17).

It is said that ravens were stealing straw from the beds of the monks at St. Cuthbert's monastery, so he rebuked them and sent them away.

They returned later, with contrite heads bowed, bringing a gift of lard as an apology.

The raven, much like the other animals we have explored, becomes an agent of grace and a sacramental sign of God's presence.

The Practice of Ecstasy and Union

Ekstasis—to stand outside of oneself, to be drawn beyond oneself into some larger reality.

—Douglas Christie, *The Blue Sapphire of the Mind*

Ecstasy may call to mind strange images of illegal drugs or, as in the Christian tradition, someone out of control with emotion or rapture. In fact, ecstasy was often experienced by many of the Christian mystics, and that experience of rapture is our natural birthright. I believe ecstasy has been dismissed by many religious institutions because it is not an experience than can be controlled. The very nature of ecstasy is to lose control, to move past your own boundaries and experience a sense of union with creation, with God, or with another human being.

Reflect for a moment on your own experiences of ecstasy. Perhaps they came while standing in a pine forest or on the peak of a mountain; maybe it was the moment of holding a beloved in sweet rest. Maybe you have tasted ecstasy in beholding an infant (your own, a grandchild, or the child of another), and you suddenly knew yourself connected, no longer separate. Or perhaps it was in releasing yourself to the sometimes exquisite freedom of dance, and realizing for a moment that there was no self-consciousness, that you were simply creation itself dancing. Or it is possible you don't have any memory of ecstatic moments, and maybe a grief rises up at ways you have held yourself back from these experiences. Whatever your experience, honor it; bring compassion and curiosity to yourself.

The mystical tradition is clear that the state of ecstasy—when the human person is caught up into union with the Divine—is considered highly favorable. Jungian analyst Robert A. Johnson wrote a book about ecstasy, describing it as the psychology of joy. The word *ecstasy* has become synonymous with joyous exaltation, and yet we might often find ourselves holding back. Sometimes joy is just as difficult to fully experience as grief or anger because there is a sense of moving beyond oneself and losing some control, of giving ourselves over to the joy that we resist. We sometimes believe we don't deserve this kind of unbridled joy, or perhaps we feel suspicious when things are going well, waiting for the next thing to fall apart rather than experiencing the joy of the moment.

Allow yourself time to surrender yourself to an experience of ecstasy and union with creation. Allow your own boundaries to soften, and see yourself as part of the natural world. Observe the places where you see nature reveling in her own kind of ecstasy, whether a dog playing with abandon or trees swaying in the wind.

Scripture Reflection
from John Valters Paintner

Praise for God's Universal Glory (Psalm 148:7–12)

Praise the LORD from the earth,
you sea monsters and all deeps,

fire and hail, snow and frost,
stormy wind fulfilling his command!

Mountains and all hills,
fruit trees and all cedars!

Wild animals and all cattle,
creeping things and flying birds!

Kings of the earth and all peoples,
princes and all rulers of the earth!

Young men and women alike,
old and young together!
—Psalm 148:7-12

Tradition tells us that King David is the author of many of the psalms. Based on linguistic analysis and a close reading of the contents, even some of the psalms which claim in their opening verse to be "a Psalm of David" may not be composed by his hand. Perhaps the king commissioned some. Or maybe David simply inspired a whole new genre of liturgical and sacred texts.

It's certainly an interesting theoretical debate, but it hardly matters one way or another for our purposes here. And that is because the psalms speak of a universal experience. When our own words fail us in prayer, the psalms can speak for us. They sing of a truth that we already know but may not be able to articulate on our own.

On occasion, there can be a sense of ease in knowing that someone else is in charge and leading the way. I don't have to come up with the words that capture the connectedness of all things or the unity I feel with all creation. It's already been done in the psalms and by the saints (and is still being done by talented writers).

Psalm 148 is one prayer for which I am particularly grateful. Despite being a trained theologian and teacher, I'm not one for telling others to pray or for leading liturgical services. And so having a psalm like this helps to fill in my spiritual gaps.

It reminds me that not just humans but all creatures (even the "sea monsters") are part of God's creation. Even the lashing rain and bitter cold are part of divine handiwork. It grounds me and puts me in right relationship to the world.

Like the author of Psalm 148, many of the prophets, when calling God's people to task for their transgressions, would call on others to bear witness. Some prophets called on other nations. Some called forth animals. And still others called upon the very heavens and earth to bear witness.

Normally, when we think of sacraments, we think of human rituals and ceremonies. Fortunately there is an increasing movement of people who refer to forests as cathedrals or bird songs as hymns. But this is not new. The Bible and early monastic writings are full of such metaphors. The real trick, the thing that still catches me out, is the realization that they aren't analogies or metaphors. These "metaphors" are the proper and original way of understanding all creation.

Before there were human forms of spiritual sacramental expression, there was creation. Our prayers, our liturgies, and our attempts to understand and express our theological understanding all originate in our observation and appreciation of what God reveals through nature. Nature is the original sacrament that reflects God's presence.

Seeing nature as the original sacrament does not mean doing away with institutional churches or formal sacraments or even rote prayers. The enduring universality of the psalms is a testament to their usefulness in modern spirituality—providing us with words when we lack them. But what we mustn't do is think that these human creations have surpassed or replaced the revelatory role of nature. Nature continues to be sacramental, a conduit that connects us to the Divine.

Meditation: Contemplate a Hazelnut

St. Julian of Norwich, a fourteenth-century anchorite in England, had a series of visions she called *Showings of Divine Love*. In one of these visions she contemplated a hazelnut closely:

> And in this he showed me something small, no bigger than a hazelnut, lying in the palm of my hand, and I perceived that it was round as any ball. I looked at it and thought: What can this be? And I was given this general answer: It is everything which is made. I was amazed that it could last, for I thought that it was so little that it could suddenly fall into nothing. And I was answered in my understanding: It lasts and always will because God loves it; and thus everything has being through the love of God.[5]

In her contemplation, she saw three aspects to the hazelnut—that God created it, God loved it, and God preserved it. This teaching showed her creation and humanity as macrocosm and microcosm. Just as God creates and sustains all of nature with love, so we are sustained as well. Perhaps just as significant, a simple hazelnut becomes the source of divine revelation.

I invite you into a meditation with a hazelnut or something equally small from creation. It could be a stone you carried home, a flower, a feather, an acorn, a nut, a leaf, or anything that you are able to hold in your hand.

Find a quiet place and turn off all distractions. Slow down and deepen your breathing. Allow yourself to fully arrive to this moment. Imagine calling back all the attention and thoughts your mind has extended out into the world. Drop your awareness down into your heart center.

Behold the object in your hand. Gaze upon it with wonder and curiosity. Marvel at its intricacies. Spend a few moments growing more intimate with its texture, color, shape, and smell. Look at it from all angles. Ask, like Julian of Norwich, "What can this be?" and listen for a response to rise up. Imagine where it came from and how it arrived to you.

See this object as the sacrament that it is, a window into the divine nature and Divine Presence. How does this shift your relationship to the object? Does it become a subject? See if you might release any barriers between you and what you hold. See yourself in this item. Ask what it has to teach you about yourself and about God. What wisdom does it have for you?

Gently bring yourself back to the room you are in by deepening your breath. Allow some time to journal any thoughts or discoveries.

Contemplative Walk: Gerard Manley Hopkins's *Inscape*

> The world is charged with the grandeur of God.
>> It will flame out, like shining from shook foil;
>> It gathers to a greatness, like the ooze of oil

Crushed. Why do men then now not reck his rod?

Generations have trod, have trod, have trod;
    And all is seared with trade; bleared, smeared with toil;
    And wears man's smudge and shares man's smell: the soil

Is bare now, nor can foot feel, being shod.

And for all this, nature is never spent;
    There lives the dearest freshness deep down things;

And though the last lights off the black West went
    Oh, morning, at the brown brink eastward, springs—

Because the Holy Ghost over the bent
    World broods with warm breast and with ah! bright
    wings.
    —Gerard Manley Hopkins, "God's Grandeur"[6]

Gerard Manley Hopkins was a Jesuit priest and poet in the nineteenth century. As a poet and priest he was deeply concerned with God's immanent presence and revelation of the divine nature in the world, essentially the sacramentality of things. One of the concepts Hopkins wrote about in his journals was that of *inscape*. Inscape is the inner nature of a thing that conveys its essence and reveals in a moment the unity of all creation. "As a name for that 'individually-distinctive' form (made up of various sense-data) which constitutes the rich and revealing 'oneness' of the natural object, he coined the word inscape."[7] Everything has an essence that points to God's nature and its connection to all of creation.

You are invited to read the poem "God's Grandeur" twice slowly before going out for a contemplative walk. Carry that first line with you: "The world is charged with the grandeur of God." Look for the ways the world flames out before you, moments that shimmer or seem luminous. In those moments, look for the *inscape*, or essence of it. Ask how it might teach you about God. Greet everything as a sacrament. Receive each moment as gift.

When you return home, allow some time to write about what you
noticed or discovered.

Herbal Invitation: Rosemary Salt or Sugar Scrub

Rosemary is one of my favorite herbs, as it has long been associated with
remembrance. Sometimes a sprig of rosemary is placed in a coffin or on
a grave as a symbol of hope that the person's memory will continue on.
Scientific studies show that the scent of rosemary does actually boost
memory. Physiologically, it helps the brain with cognitive function. On a
spiritual level, it helps with remembering those who have gone before us
or with remembering what is most important in our lives.

You are invited to make a rosemary scrub, which can be used to release and renew your body. If you don't have rosemary, you can substitute
another herb and essential oil.

Begin as always with some time for prayer and centering. Set a sacred
intention for the creation of this scrub. Name what you want to remember
and honor. Name your own desire for release.

In a large bowl mix together one cup of sea salt or white sugar and
one-quarter cup of either fresh or dried rosemary needles. Pour one-quarter cup of a skin-safe oil—almond or jojoba work well in this—over the
ingredients. Then using a spoon, blend everything together. You can add
more oil if the texture feels like it needs it. Finally add five to seven drops
of rosemary essential oil if desired, and be sure to mix well once again.

After you've made the scrub, take a bath with candles lit. Allow this
to be a time of prayer. Inhale the fragrance and call to mind your ancestors, asking for their support and protection. Remember that oil is often
used to anoint recipients of sacraments, so feel the connection to this
sacramental act.

Beginning with the soles of your feet, gently and lovingly apply the
scrub in slow circular motions, offering some massage to your body.
Move from the feet to the legs, to hips and belly, to chest, to arms and
neck. As you scrub, imagine what you want to release during this season
of life. If grief arises, let that flow as well.

Visual Art Exploration: Mirroring Nature

For this visual exploration, I invite you to begin by spending some time in nature. You will want to find a quiet place without a lot of people going by; it could be a park in the early morning, a riverside, a seashore, or even a backyard. I invite you to approach various aspects of nature and mirror them with your body. If you see a tree, you might spend a few minutes trying to embody "treeness" and mirror how the tree moves with your own body. This doesn't have to be an exact representation. The idea is to enter into relationship with the tree and imagine how it feels inside, and then move in whatever way seems reflective of that. Allow some time for this relationship to unfold; when it feels like enough, take some deep breaths and have a physical connection for a moment. You might lean against the tree or place your hands on its bark, offering gratitude, saying, "You are sacrament."

Then move to the next thing in nature calling to you. This time it might be some grass, a bird, or the water lapping the shore. For each of these, allow a few minutes to really enter into an embodied connection with whatever you are mirroring. Imagine entering into the reality of this being; let the shape or movement arise from that place of connection. When you feel done, spend a few moments just resting in stillness, and then make a physical connection and give thanks for the sacrament of this moment.

Once you have moved through this experience, having three or four connections, spend some time journaling to notice what you felt and discovered. Take some colored pens, pencils, crayons, or markers and some plain paper. Draw the essence of what you experienced with each encounter. Let the image be a representation in color and shape of what you discovered through this way of connecting.

Writing Exploration: When I Despair

> When despair for the world grows in me
> and I wake in the night at the least sound
> in fear of what my life and my children's lives may be,
> I go and lie down where the wood drake

> rests in his beauty on the water, and the great heron
>   feeds.
> I come into the peace of wild things
> who do not tax their lives with forethought
> of grief. I come into the presence of still water.
> And I feel above me the day-blind stars
> waiting with their light. For a time
> I rest in the grace of the world, and am free.
> —Wendell Berry, "The Peace of Wild Things"[8]

Read the poem through at least twice, and let yourself linger with his images.

A great way to find inspiration for a poem is to take or adapt a line from another poem as a place to begin. In your journal, write the words "When I despair," and then continue writing with your own images. See what wants to emerge in response.

Anytime you feel stuck, write those words again, "When I despair," so they become a mantra throughout the poem. Each time you write the words, allow new images to come forth. They don't all have to connect to one another. Once you come to a place where it feels complete, read your poem over and resist the urge to edit.

Previous Participant Poems

When I Despair

When I despair I give myself the luxury of tears.
Oh, who am I kidding?
The tears wash out of me and over me and through me.
but then it *is* me who hastens to grab back control and
what I presume to be my dignity.
"Pray, Bethie, pray," I command myself
as I reach for a cookie, a chocolate—but never a drink.
When I despair I'd rather feel the pain,
the whip-like tongues that bite my shoulder.

When I despair,
I reach for my jacket and my camera and head on down the road.
I seek the earthy smell of woods and to hear Mother in the creek.
But, maybe more telling, is that "I head down the road."
When I despair, I do my utmost
to outrun
to board the train
to climb the tree
to jump into the current
to fly.
Anything but curl up inside myself.

—Beth Almond Ford

When despair clogs my psychic arteries
like a cold-growing virus
and I stare at the blank screen of life,
I step out
and peer at the stars,
let the chill of light years zooming past
over my head
transport me—
let myself be enfolded
by this creation
so big
so wise
so true.

—Melissa Campbell Langdell

When I Despair . . .

When I despair I imagine reaching
for another's hand
in the dark.

When I despair, I light a candle
in a red votive, because I know
faraway someone else does the same.
Perhaps in some small way,
our prayer encircles the world.

When I despair,
I think of the hills
where the light never glares,
the salted fog returns every morning.
And I can draw back pieces of myself
that scattered.
In ridge shadows,
I search for a dappled horse
and the place
where it becomes real from a dream.

—Sherry Weaver Smith

Closing Blessing

In this chapter we explored Earth as the original sacrament. There is a
sense of God's incarnate presence in creation that shimmers forth to reveal the holiness of all things. Notice how your senses come alive when
you walk out in the world aware of its sacramental nature. What do your
eyes, ears, noise, mouth, and skin each reveal to you about how God is
alive in the world around you?

Blessings . . .

Bless you happy-faced pansies who I walked by every day with-
out noticing . . .
Bless you busy bee just going about your bee-ness . . .
Bless you purple flowers joyfully waving in the wind . . .
Bless you darting bird moving freely with such great delight . . .
Bless you delightful wind who is making my goose bumps rise . . .

Bless you broken, damaged, majestic, powerful tree . . .
Bless you bird-song for blanketing the world with your life-giving, joyous cacophony . . .

—Betty Meadows

CHAPTER 7

EARTH AS THE ORIGINAL LITURGY

Religion has always kept earth time. Liturgy only gives sanction to what the heart already knows.

–Phyllis Tickle, *Phyllis Tickle: Essential Spiritual Writings*[1]

In the opening pages of *Being Still: Reflections on an Ancient Mystical Tradition*, Jean-Yves Leloup tells the story of a young monk who comes to Fr. Seraphim to learn about prayer of the heart.[2] Fr. Seraphim says that before he teaches him this way of prayer, the young monk must learn to meditate like a mountain. The young monk learns stability of posture and grounding from the mountain, the weight of presence, and the experience of calmness and stability. He enters into the timeless time of mountains and experiences eternity within and around him while also learning the grace of the seasons.

Next Fr. Seraphim sends him to learn how to meditate like a poppy, taking his mountain wisdom with him. From the poppy he learns to turn himself toward the light and to orient his meditation practice from his inner depths toward radiance. The poppy also teaches him both uprightness and the ability to bend with the wind. And while the mountain taught him about the eternal, the poppy teaches him about the finitude of our days as the blossom begins to wither. He learns that meditation means experiencing the eternal in each fleeting moment.

He is then sent to the ocean to learn the wisdom of ebbing and flowing. He learns to synchronize his breath with the "great breathing rhythm of the waves." As he floats on the sea he also discovers the great calmness of the sea below its undulating surface, and he learns to hold awareness of his own distinct self without being carried away by the rhythm of breathing.

Fr. Seraphim finally has him learn to pray like a bird, saying that the prophet Isaiah describes meditation as the cry of an animal like the roaring of a lion or the song of a dove (see Is 31:4; 38:14). The bird is to teach him how to sing continuously, repeating the name of God in his heart without ceasing. The invocation of the Divine Name leads him to a deep place of stillness.

Earth and her creatures teach us how to pray, how to worship and praise, but only if we listen and pay attention to their rhythms in this world.

Monks know this rhythm well, as the ancient practice of the Liturgy of the Hours immerses them in the rise and fall of each day. On this liturgical rhythm, Thomas Berry writes, "From an early period Christians adopted a liturgy that carefully observed the correspondences of human praise with the numinous moments of the dawn and sunset and with the transitions of the various seasons of the year. This liturgy was carried out most faithfully in the Benedictine and Cistercian monasteries of Europe up through the medieval period. The social order was itself governed by this basic rhythm of life."[3] The threshold times of day, especially dawn and dusk, have long been considered numinous—times of special awe as the world moves from light to dark or dark to light. This fundamental rhythm is the foundation of this prayer practice and reveals Earth as the original liturgy.

Creation in Continual Praise

The fire has its flame and praises God. The wind blows the flame and praises God. In the voice we hear the word which praises God. And the word, when heard, praises God. So all of creation is a song of praise to God.

—St. Hildegard of Bingen

The Hebrew and Christian scriptures present us with a vision of nature whose primary function is to engage in a continual act of praising the Divine. Contemplatives who wish to learn how to follow St. Paul's invitation to "pray without ceasing" (1 Thes 5:17) would do well to pay attention to the natural world.

Each time you go for a walk, see if you can begin with a sense that you are stepping into a landscape that is animate and alive, that is participating in the great unfolding of a liturgy of praise. Then let your body join in with this ongoing hymn, knowing your body is intimate with this already ongoing song. We have separated ourselves from creation by claiming consciousness only for ourselves. All elements of creation participate in this primordial cathedral, scriptures, saints, spiritual directors, icon, sacrament, and liturgy offering wisdom to us with each turn. These sacred places of encounter with the Divine are profoundly embodied.

The psalms see all of creation itself as offering continual praise to God. The sea, the sky, the trees, the animals, the stars—all these are seen to be singing God's glory without human words but with another kind of language. All of creation is called to praise the sacredness of all things, never exhausting this possibility. The psalms exhort, "Let everything that breathes praise the LORD!" (Ps 150:6). This is a continual and ever-unfolding chorus of celebration happening all around us, and we are invited to join. Praise should arise from our hearts as spontaneously as it does from pines and panthers, from the sea and sloths.

In an old Irish poem about a mistle thrush, the bird is celebrated for its beauty and described as giving an "impromptu sermon"[4] that teaches his listeners much about the goodness of God. The bird is not only sacrament but also preacher and liturgist, offering his own perspective on celebration of the Divine Source.

There is a wonderful story about St. Brendan the Navigator, who traveled miles and miles by sea in search of the land promised to the saints. Along the way, he stopped at many different islands, and on one he encountered a group of white birds who sang the psalms in praise of God at the appointed hours of the day. These birds were the original monks, already singing the Divine Office.

The psalms of praise often describe nature as alive and in perpetual celebration. Thomas Merton saw his call as a monk to listen for the song being sung through all of creation. He was invited to join in with this original liturgy already happening all around him. In the forest he could tend to "the sweet songs of living things,"[5] whose celebratory choirs he joined. In these moments he touched the paradise that pulses all around us.

In *Way of the Pilgrim*, a nineteenth-century Russian Orthodox text, it is written, "And while I prayed in the depths of the heart, everything around me seemed transformed: the trees, grass, birds, earth, air, light—every created thing seemed to proclaim that it bears witness to God's love for humanity. Everything was praying. Everything sang glory be to God."[6] All of nature sings glory to God, even the seasons themselves. The liturgical calendar reflects the seasonal cycle of dying and rising. Nature has her own liturgy, which we discover when we begin to anticipate the return of the salmon each fall in the Pacific Northwest, the migration of swans and geese each winter flocking by the thousands, the first snowdrops growing in Ireland as a sign of spring, and the lush bounty of fruits and vegetables that arrives each summer around the world. These are feast days in the calendar of creation's unfolding, times to celebrate as nature offers up her signs of what is to come. Even the sun's return each morning elicits the birds to sing their praises.

Feeding the Birds

These past couple of years I have fallen in love with birds. I have always been an admirer of crows with their thick glossy feathers and their intelligence. Perhaps because we moved to a home with a south-facing patio, it seems as if we have more variety of avian visitors now than we ever have before. I have to admit that while I admire the seagulls for their resiliency and love of playing in the wind, I find them a bit aggressive and try to dissuade them from landing on our balcony. Pigeons I can tolerate a bit better, but again, they can also be a bit aggressive with one another.

However, I have fallen in love with starlings, sparrows, and wagtails, the smaller, shier birds who need a bit of encouragement. Part of the liturgy of my mornings is to put out the bird seed and wait and watch them arrive one by one. In May, starlings nest in the bush outside our building, and their cries fill the air for weeks as the younger ones follow their parents with mouths wide open.

The birds that visit our home remind me again of the scripture verse in which Jesus reminds us to look to the birds of the air and not be anxious about where our provision will come from (see Mt 6:25–34). God is sometimes compared to a mother bird sheltering her young or an eagle in flight. The act of feeding the birds calls me back to a deep trust in God's presence and to find that presence in wild places. The birds arrive each morning in their own liturgy, singing me awake. We can turn ourselves inside out with worry about tomorrow, but time spent in nature often gives us a new perspective—one that reminds us of the endurance of things and the rhythms that surround us.

St. Brigid and the Oystercatchers

There are many stories about St. Brigid's kinship with animals. She is perhaps best known for her white cow that was her companion and provided an endless supply of milk to all who needed it. She also had a close kinship with oystercatchers, seabirds found along the coast of Ireland and Scotland. The Gaelic name for these birds is *Giolla Brid*, which means "Brigid's servants."

One story tells of how Brigid was on the run from those who would do her harm. She reached the shoreline and collapsed onto the sand, as she was trapped and could go no further. The oystercatchers saw her plight and covered her with sand, seaweed, and shells so that her pursuers were not able to find her and passed her by. I love this story of intimacy with creation and the sheer joy and gratitude that Brigid must have felt in response to her helpers. This sense of profound connection with nature informs our own liturgies of praise.

The Practice of Paradise

In the monastic tradition, there is great emphasis on the dream of paradise and the insistence that the world has been and will once again be whole.

In fact, the world, even in its apparently degraded condition, is already complete in its wholeness—we just have to slow down to see it and cherish it. This is the heart of the contemplative tradition: cultivating a way of vision that sees beneath the surface of things and discovers the Sacred shimmering in all moments. Creation is a sacred liturgy singing us toward paradise and reminding us of our own potential and holy direction.

Remember for a moment the quote from Thomas Merton we opened this book with: "Living the life of the new creation in which the right relation to all the rest of God's creatures is fully restored."[7] In part we do this by practicing paradise—practicing seeing beneath the surface of things to the Sacred within them—and remembering that there is what Merton calls a "hidden wholeness" that is present to us if we only have eyes to see the greening power alive in the world.

We can come to know Earth as whole in this moment, while also acknowledging the great work we must do to restore the wholeness out of the destruction we have wrought.

Practicing paradise is one way to restore wholeness and is built on the idea of a "life free from care" or a life without purpose. This does not mean a life without meaning, but instead a life that is not burdened by our human desire to make heroic victories from our lives. It means living with a purpose vastly different than what society thinks is valuable.

Living a "life free from care" is a significant theme in the ancient Christian contemplative texts, originating with Jesus' call on the Sermon on the Mount to live free from anxiety. He expresses it perhaps most clearly in his words about the "birds of the air" and the "lilies of the field" (see Mt 6:25–31; John reflected on this passage in chapter 3). These images would have come alive for the early monks as they sought to live unburdened by daily concerns, free of what the world said was most important.

The early monks longed, as most of us do, to live in a way that was unburdened by anxiety and fear. All of their spiritual practices were in service to this ultimate goal. They longed to be healed of the internal divisions that kept them from seeing the abundant grace freely offered moment by moment and that could be heard by listening to the liturgy and song of creation.

To live in paradise in the midst of this world means to see things differently. This can only come through practice. Theologian Douglas Christie writes, "At its root, this is an eschatological vision, born of a recognition that the world as we know it is broken and frayed but that it is possible to discern even in the midst of such brokenness . . . the true, unbroken character of the world that is always mysteriously present. The capacity to cultivate an awareness of this 'hidden wholeness' and to live within and on behalf of it is one of the contemplative tradition's primary contributions to the work of healing of the world."[8] Our presence as contemplatives in the world—seeking to overcome dualism and divisions, longing to see the wholeness that is already present within us and in the world around us—is the work of healing the world. It is because we have cultivated our capacity to see that we live into a way of being that is free from anxiety and bears witness to an alternative. Liturgy celebrates the wholeness that is already in our midst.

Scripture Reflection
from John Valters Paintner

God the Creator and Provider (Psalm 104)

Bless the LORD, O my soul.
> O LORD my God, you are very great.
You are clothed with honor and majesty,
> wrapped in light as with a garment.
You stretch out the heavens like a tent,
> you set the beams of your chambers on the waters,
you make the clouds your chariot,
> you ride on the wings of the wind,
you make the winds your messengers,
> fire and flame your ministers. . . .

May the glory of the LORD endure forever;
>   may the LORD rejoice in his works—
who looks on the earth and it trembles,
>   who touches the mountains and they smoke.
I will sing to the LORD as long as I live;
>   I will sing praise to my God while I have being.
May my meditation be pleasing to him,
>   for I rejoice in the LORD.
Let sinners be consumed from the earth,
>   and let the wicked be no more.
Bless the LORD, O my soul.
Praise the LORD!

—Psalm 104:1-4, 31-35

It is not just humans who reflect and praise God's majesty. We are but one (although often loud and self-centered) part of God's creation. Psalm 104 is a beautiful reminder of how creation praises God's majesty as the psalm describes the unending liturgy of all nature.

The very structure of the psalm is a retelling of the first creation myth. The opening stanzas begin with the separation of light and dark, of the waters above and the waters below. Next, the psalmist writes of the springs and streams that allow the animals to quench their thirst and that water the vegetation. The vegetation gives shelter and sustenance to the creatures of land and air. Even the innumerable and unknown creatures of the sea are mentioned. The final stanzas remind us that all of creation is sustained by God's hand.

One of the things I love about this particular psalm is that it reinforces the original poetic nature of the first creation myth. The authors of that story lived centuries before not only the invention of the scientific method but also the very idea of an objective history. The authors of the first creation myth were attempting to express a deep truth about the Creator and our relationship to God.

What the psalm tells us so poetically is that the original liturgy is witnessed in creation itself. It is woven into how nature—and ourselves as a part of nature—is created to be and to celebrate. Liturgy is simply the formalized, communal expression of a natural instinct to gather and share a common spiritual experience. We would do well to turn to our fellow creatures to learn liturgy done well.

Meditation: Tree of Life

In the thirteenth century, St. Bonaventure, a Franciscan friar, wrote *The Tree of Life*,[9] which is a prayerful meditation on the life of Christ. In it, Bonaventure invites his reader to imagine the tree as a metaphor for prayer. I have adapted and expanded this prayer here, and I invite you to enter into it in your imagination.

Begin by finding a quiet place. Turn off distractions and begin to center yourself by deepening your breath. Let your breath be slow and full, and drop your awareness from your head down to your heart center. Rest there for a few moments in this sanctuary of your heart. Become present to the divine spark that the mystics tell us dwells in each of our hearts.

Visualize a lush tree; it might be a tree you know and love, or it might be a tree you have never seen before. See its roots being watered by an endless fountain that becomes a huge river that waters all the gardens surrounding it. There is an abundance of water and sunlight so that everything is flourishing.

From the trunk of this tree, see twelve strong branches extending out. Each branch is covered with leaves, flowers, and fruit. You draw closer to look at the leaves and see that they contain healing medicine, which can prevent and cure any kind of illness. You call to mind any place you need healing, whether physical, mental, or spiritual, and ask the tree to offer you just the right herbal gift. See what is offered to you, and receive it with gratitude. You might pause and imagine you can make a cup of tea with these leaves, and then slowly partake of what they offer to you. See their medicine go to whatever place in you most needs it.

Then look closely again at the tree and notice the huge array of flowers garnishing the branches—flowers of every color and scent imaginable. Pause at each one and gently breathe in its fragrance, savoring the smell. Let it waft over and around you so that you stand in a heavenly cloud of beautiful fragrance.

Then turn one more time to the branches, and notice the fruits ripening on the branches. There are twelve different kinds of fruits at peak sweetness. You choose one to eat and savor the taste, letting its juice run down your chin. You know that you could eat these fruits for the rest of your life and never tire of their delicious flavors. You feel the nourishment reaching every part of you, renewing you in body and spirit.

You spend a few minutes simply resting with your back to the trunk, feeling the solidness of the tree and its support for you. You soak in gratitude for healing medicine, for fragrance that lifts the heart, and for the tastes that deeply nourish you for the road ahead. You offer a prayer of blessing and thanksgiving, knowing this tree awaits you in your heart anytime you are in need. You hear the birds around you singing their joy. Sit with the liturgy of praise unfolding within and around you.

Gently deepen your breath again, and slowly bring your awareness back to the room. Allow a few minutes for journaling, to notice anything in particular that shimmered for you or surprised you.

Contemplative Walk: Receiving Blessing

Begin by breathing deeply and centering yourself. As you walk in the world, feel yourself a part of the divine liturgy unfolding at every moment, and ask nature to bless you. With each step become aware of what is around you. Become present to the birds, the plants, the sky, the wind, and the trees. Ask each of these elements of nature to gift you with a blessing as you go forth. Ask creation to bless your own places of birthing, that they may rise up with joy to meet a world in need.

Pause regularly to receive the blessings being offered to you. When you return home, allow some time to write down what you discovered and received.

Herbal Invitation: Herb-Infused Honey

Another way to work with herbs is by infusing them with honey. You could use organic dried rose petals again or another herb. Thyme, lavender, and rosemary all work well for this as they are quite aromatic. Honey is the labor of thousands of bees and offers us the gift of sweetness and the essence of the land where the bees were working. Look for a local supplier of honey if possible, and have a jar handy along with a small bowl for mixing and a spoon.

Begin by pausing to center yourself and to bless your intentions for this time.

The process to make infused honey is very similar to the one for infused oil. Place the dried herbs in the jar; fill the jar with honey. Stir to remove air bubbles and to make sure the herbs are completely covered. Add more honey if needed.

Allow the honey to infuse for at least one week. You can then either strain the herbs from the honey or serve with the herbs included, as they are edible.

When we do our closing ritual for one of our Ireland pilgrimages, we use honey as a symbol for savoring the sweetness of life. Each pilgrim takes a slice of apple, which is one of the sacred trees in Ireland and also a symbol of paradise, and we dip the apple into the honey, taking time to really taste all of the flavors. Similarly, you can create your own liturgy to celebrate Earth and incorporate the honey as a sign of nature's sweet gifts. You can also just take a spoonful anytime your heart needs a reminder of life's sweetness.

Visual Art Exploration: Liturgy for Earth

Michael Meade, a storyteller and mythologist in the Pacific Northwest, once said that we can never know whether our efforts are actually making a difference—for Earth, or in another person's life—but that it is essential that we make the effort. Our commitment to spiritual practice itself, even in the face of despairing news each day, is an act of hope and a contribution to the transformation happening in the silence of things.

You are invited to create a liturgy for Earth. Gather together prayers and poems that are meaningful for you. Include some time for lament and grieving Earth's suffering. Play music that connects you to Earth, whether songs about creation or the songs of creation such as the songs of humpback whales or the sound of ocean waves. Include a ritual act, some physical embodiment of your commitment to the natural world.

You might let this liturgy arise spontaneously on a day when you are out walking, noticing what words or songs arise in your heart, following your own impulse to offer some gesture to Earth in prayer, letting yourself sink into moments of sorrow, and savoring moments of wonder. You don't have to plan it out; you can let your body lead you in its discovery.

Written Exploration: Blessing for Creation

At the close of each chapter there has been a blessing for creation written by previous participants in our retreats and online programs. Now I invite you to write your own blessing. Spend some time outdoors and see what words come to you. A blessing is a way of offering gratitude and lifting up what God has already blessed. It is an act of acknowledgment and wonder. Offer gratitude in your blessing for each leaf, twig, blossom, stone, and creature. Celebrate the liturgy of praise these gifts of nature elicit in your own heart.

Previous Participant Poems

May the holy being-ness of Mother Earth bless you with unexpected paths and hidden treasures,
secret visions and moist grass after a summer rain.
May your life be as blessed as a field of wildflowers arrayed in all the colors of the rainbow,
and may all your weeds have lacy leaves and curious crawling bugs.
May your spaces be thin and healing,
may doorways always beckon you, may your climbing vines and ancient stones and flowers bloom for love of life.
Bless your delicate blossoming and the blue-gray sky.

—Cris Davis

Did I ever thank you properly,
sister digitalis, for your service
to my infant son and the others
born with different hearts?
Your blessed purpose,
dear perfect, speckled vessel,
to keep them alive.

—Ani Tuzman

Bless you redwood tree
for your ministry of strength and
courage for growing and offering seed . . .
Bless you wild roses for your
joy, beauty, and sweet fragrance
delighting each passerby,
reminding us to slow down
and embrace our own beauty . . .

Bless the pheasants for their morning song and dance
challenging us to wake up and listen . . .

Bless the delicate flowers of the garden dancing in the wind
with all of their variety and color.

Bless the herbs for the gifts of healing and wisdom,
for their scents, and love and protection.

Bless the yew trees for their gifts of teaching me to love as a
    young child,
and for the hope and solace they provided.

—Sharie Bowman

Bless the fresh bedlinen, flopping into place
Bless the open hearts and enfolding embrace
Bless the bird song—insistent yet light as air

Bless this buttercup reaching for light
Bless this gusting wind lifting the leaves; stirring my soul
Bless this fallen tree—potential nursing log
Nurturing; nourishing whilst slowly returning to Mother earth.

—Melitta Bosworth

Closing Blessing

In this chapter we explored Earth as the original liturgy and all creation praising God all around us at all times. The psalms and scriptures are clear on this; it is we humans who are learning from nature how to give proper glory to God.

Blessing of the Ordinary Extraordinary

Bless the unfurling, the outstretching
branches of the monkey puzzle tree.
May we reflect their curiosity and desire for life in all its fullness.

Bless the swifts flexibly flying,
finding sustenance hour by hour, day by day,
May we also be nourished by nature's riches.

Bless the bright fallen poppy leaves
vibrancy of Spirit lying waiting
May we let them cradle us into stillness and new life

Bless the lichened branch glowing on the tree
life intermingling with death
May we be aware and enriched by the paths of life and death.

Bless the large allium head with so much to give
perfect fecundity laying open
May we be willing to let go and share our own goodness.

Bless all of God's wonder-full creation
where everything belongs
May we be delighted day by day and know that God is good.

—Marianne Anker-Peterson

CONCLUSION

Love all God's creation, the whole and every grain of sand
in it. Love every leaf, every ray of God's light. Love the animals,
love the plants, love everything. If you love everything, you will
perceive the divine mystery in things. . . . When you are left
alone, pray. Love to throw yourself on the earth and kiss it.
Kiss the earth and love it with an unceasing, consuming love.

–Fyodor Dostoevsky, *The Karamazov Brothers*[1]

Our lives tend to be very domesticated. We have artificial lights that illumine the dark nights. We have heating and air conditioning to adjust the climate indoors. When we travel we can cross oceans in a matter of hours. These are all good things for which we can be grateful. But as we come to the end of this book, we might also reflect on the ways we insulate ourselves from the world outside and the impact this has on us.

Our lives are domesticated in other ways too. We often live our lives to please others or to live up to their expectations. We fall into the cultural trap of determining our value by what we do or produce. Midlife comes as a time to reevaluate our priorities and how we want to spend the precious gift of time each of us has been given. Nature has a way of reminding us of some of the deeper longings in our heart that have nothing to do with status or wealth, and everything to do with exploring the wild edges of our being and of the Divine. Our images of God become domesticated, and spending time in creation can remind us of the wild God who breathes new life into us and disrupts our plans.

Let's return for a moment to the practice I invited you to in the first chapter of participating in the life of creation. Call to mind again the feeling of your skin touching the grass, the intimacy with creation and what it evoked for you. Return to this experience if possible.

Remember to give yourself over to time spent simply being outside in the presence of living, breathing plants and animals. Let your heart receive their song. Let your body join in.

Dostoevsky's words speak to me of an extravagance that I wish for each of us. What would it be like to love so generously without holding back? How might you be transformed by softening yourself so completely? What would it be like to throw yourself on the earth and kiss it?

In the introduction, I shared Charles Eisenstein's call to a revolution of love. I believe this is the only way that love can take deep root in our hearts. The stories of the mystics show this path forward. Theology keeps us in endless analysis: "The first task before us, that which theology can assist, is to revision all beings as united in their createdness, given to one another as companions, sacraments of 'the love that moves the sun and other stars.'"[2]

This is not a contained love, one that we keep within boundaries, but a wild love that springs up from the deep creative and spontaneous recesses of our hearts. The wild instinct that Earth and her creatures reveal to us so freely reminds us of our own instinctual being, that part of ourselves where we feel most alive, most creative, and most free.

Thomas Berry writes, "First, we must understand that the universe is a communion of subjects, not a collection of objects. This implies that we recover our primordial intimacy with the entire natural world. We belong here."[3] A revolution of love, a renewal of our primordial intimacy with the world, a reclamation of our inner wildness—these are the holy directions we are being called in, directions that we can't think our way into but can only move toward as we yield to the longings of the heart.

A New Pentecost

John Philip Newell, in his book *A New Harmony*, describes this human awakening to Earth's intimacy with us as a "new Pentecost."[4] This new Pentecost is one that is happening all around us in every moment. There is a continual emergence through the inspiration of the Spirit as we recognize our unity with creation; we are coming to know that we are not separate from creation, that instead we are earthed and wild. We are discovering that Earth has everything to teach us about the spiritual journey from liturgy, to daily prayer, to sanctuary space, to the scriptures. It is all there already for us—we simply need to enter into communion with it.

Newell asks the question, "A new and vast Pentecost is stirring in the human soul. How will we serve it?"[5] One way, I suggest, is by embracing your own wildness. The Spirit is the epitome of this wild energy at work in the world, the One to break down boundaries and move us to the edges of our known lives and call us beyond into something new. Our work as contemplatives and spiritual seekers is to recover the spiritual power of our own wild nature.

Scripture Reflection from John Valters Paintner

Pentecost and the Coming of the Holy Spirit (Acts of the Apostles 2:1–31)

> When the day of Pentecost had come, they were all together in one place. And suddenly from heaven there came a sound like the rush of a violent wind, and it filled the entire house where they were sitting. Divided tongues, as of fire, appeared among them, and a tongue rested on each of them. All of them were filled with the Holy Spirit and began to speak in other languages, as the Spirit gave them ability.
>
> —Acts 2:1-4

Most people know of Pentecost as the birth of the Christian Church. In the Christian calendar, this holy day celebrates the time when the apostles, filled with the Holy Spirit, preach the Gospel message publicly for the first time. We commemorate the day the Twelve left their place of hiding to go out among the large crowds gathered in Jerusalem.

Jews from all over the known world in the holy city of David were there that day to celebrate the original Jewish religious festival, known in Hebrew as *Shavuot*. This Jewish Festival of Weeks (seven weeks after Passover) commemorates the giving of the Torah to Moses on Mount Sinai during the Exodus experience. Agriculturally speaking, as several major Jewish festivals coincide and relate to yearly agricultural events, Pentecost is the time of year for the first fruit harvest. A tithe from this harvest would have been brought to the Temple in Jesus' day by observant Jews, hence the large international gathering of Jews in Jerusalem on this particular day.

Even prior to the Roman occupation of the Holy Land, the Jews had been conquered and dispersed by several previous invaders. The descendants of Abraham and Sarah, in the first century AD, were a scattered people. For generations, these Jews would have been slowly adapting to their new homelands with their different languages and customs. And yet many of them continued to return to Jerusalem, when possible, for these special religious occasions.

Like the worldwide community of believers that are part of the Christian church today, there are a great many things that separate us. But our faith, our spiritual journey back home, unites us.

The Acts of the Apostles begins with the Ascension of Christ into heaven. The Resurrection has already happened, and Jesus has spent time with the disciples around the region of Judea. The apostles pick a successor to Judas, but they are still by-and-large in hiding. The possibility of arrest and execution is still their primary concern. Their faith in Jesus has been restored, but they lack the courage to do anything about it.

Then one day, on the holy feast of *Shavuot*, the apostles go from being full of fear to being full of the Holy Spirit. The sound of a violent wind enters their dwelling, blowing away their doubts and trepidations. And so there is room for them to be filled with an energy for God that manifests itself as tongues of fire on each of their heads. The newfound Spirit compels them out of hiding and into the public arena.

The apostles are so enthusiastic that someone in the crowd suggests that they are drunk. This isn't a small side snicker—Peter feels compelled to address the accusation.

Another way of interpreting the imagery of the wind and tongues of flame is to imagine the wind sweeping into the locked room and into the apostles as a mirroring of God breathing life into the first man made of clay from the Garden of Eden. I love the elements as symbols of the apostles' transformation from timid followers to bold proclaimers. They are filled with the wild spirit of God and rush past their self-imposed boundaries to new edges.

Entering the Cosmic Dance

> The Lord plays and diverts Himself in the garden of His creation, and if we could let go of our own obsession with what we think is the meaning of it all, we might be able to hear His call and follow Him in His mysterious, cosmic dance . . . we are invited to forget ourselves on purpose, cast our awful solemnity to the winds and join in the general dance.
>
> −Thomas Merton, *New Seeds of Contemplation*[6]

This is the ongoing invitation as you journey forth from this book: To let the great dance of life continue to flow through you. To know that dance as originating in the great sanctuary of praise that is creation. To feel the dance of the seasons give you permission to feel the fullness of your gifts and also the quiet rest of being.

Merton described God as "Lord of the Dance" and surmised that the things over which we obsess and analyze are probably what God thinks are least important. The dance calls us to forget ourselves, to move beyond our self-consciousness, our worries over how others perceive us, and to discover the freedom and joy that dance can bring.

As I finish writing this book, there is much to be hopeful about. The United Kingdom and the Republic of Ireland have become the first two

countries to declare climate emergencies. Greta Thunberg, the courageous and inspiring young woman who initiated the youth movement to
combat the climate crisis, is being recognized more and more for her
message. Solar, wind, and other technologies are improving at vast rates
and being installed in greater quantities than ever before. There are many
more examples of climate momentum happening now, and hopefully far
more by the time this book is published.

Closing Blessing

We bring this journey to a close, but hopefully it will also be a new beginning, a Pentecost and call to love and radical service. My deepest prayer
is that each of us goes forth with a heart kindled by love to deepen our
intimacy with Earth and to recognize the profound ways she teaches us
about God's desires for us.

> May we always remember that we belong to this beautiful Earth,
> that it will bear our sorrows and share our joys.
>
> May we be deeply rooted in our truth so that we may grow tall and
> strong as the trees, offering shelter to all who need it.
>
> May we be open to receiving our gifts and share them with others
> as freely as the rain falls, and be ever thankful.
>
> May we be radiant and natural and fragrant as flowers that flour-
> ish, nurtured by love.
>
> May we always be drawn to where the air is good and fresh and
> life-giving so that we may be en-spirited and breathe freely.
>
> May our passion for tenderness and love be kindled and burn with
> the ferocity of a campfire and the merriment of kindred souls.
>
> May each of us dare to sing our song of praise as the birds sing
> theirs, so that our songs may rise up together wherever we are.
>   —Felicity Collins

ACKNOWLEDGMENTS

Writing books is, for me, always the fruition of much reading, much pondering, and many conversations. This book in particular was also the fruit of many hours spent walking in the woods, climbing mountains, swimming in the sea, and gardening. I am especially grateful to Betsey Beckman, my longtime teaching partner and dear friend who has co-led many versions of this material (both in person and online) with groups. I am also tremendously grateful for the groups who were eager to immerse themselves in these ideas, for the reflections they shared, and especially for those who were willing to share their poems in these pages.

A book like this also requires a commitment to the lived experience of nature connection. I am grateful for living on the wild edges of Ireland, a place of stunning beauty with the sea just outside my window, mountains across the bay, and forests a short drive away. Ireland is a very elemental place and has gifted me so much in this way.

Thanks as always to the wonderful and amazing team at Ave Maria Press. This is my seventh book with them (and thirteenth overall). I feel much gratefulness for my editor, Amber Elder, and everyone involved in the book's production.

Last but not least, I always carry a heart full of gratitude for my beloved husband, John, with whom I celebrate twenty-five years of marriage this year as I am finishing the writing of this book. For always supporting me in all kinds of weather, I love you beyond measure.

ADDITIONAL RESOURCES: RECOMMENDED READING LIST

Abram, David. *Becoming Animal: An Earthly Cosmology*. New York: Vintage Books, 2010.

———. *The Spell of the Sensuous: Perception and Language in a More-Than-Human World*. New York: Vintage Books, 2010.

Atkins, Sally, and Melia Snyder. *Nature-Based Expressive Arts Therapy: Integrating the Expressive Arts and Ecotherapy*. London: Jessica Kingsley Publishers, 2018.

Berry, Thomas. *The Great Work: Our Way into the Future*. New York: Bell Tower, 1999.

———. *The Sacred Universe: Earth, Spirituality, and Religion in the Twenty-First Century*. New York: Columbia University Press, 2009.

Chase, Steven. *Nature as Spiritual Practice*. Grand Rapids, MI: Wm. B. Eerdmans, 2011.

Christie, Douglas. *The Blue Sapphire of the Mind: Notes for a Contemplative Ecology*. Oxford: Oxford University Press, 2013.

Jung, C. G. *The Earth Has a Soul: C.G. Jung on Nature, Technology, and Modern Life*. Edited by Meredith Sabini. Berkeley, CA: North Atlantic Books, 2002.

Kopytin, Alexander, and Madeline Rugh. *Environmental Expressive Therapies: Nature-Assisted Theory and Practice*. New York: Routledge, 2017.

London, Peter. *Drawing Closer to Nature: Making Art in Dialogue with the Natural World*. Boston: Shambhala, 2003.

Merton, Thomas. *When the Trees Say Nothing: Writing on Nature*. Edited by Kathleen Deignan. Notre Dame, IN: Ave Maria Press, 2015.

Olsen, Andrea, and Caryn McHose. *Body and Earth: An Experiential Guide*. Lebanon, NH: University Press of New England, 2002.

Plotkin, Bill. *Nature and the Human Soul: Cultivating Wholeness and Community in a Fragmented World*. Novato, CA: New World Library, 2007.

————. *SoulCraft: Crossing into the Mysteries of Nature and Psyche*. Novato, CA: New World Library, 2003.

————. *Wild Mind: A Field Guide to the Human Psyche*. Novato, CA: New World Library, 2013.

Stanley, Bruce. *Forest Church: A Field Guide to Spiritual Connection with Nature*. Vestal, NY: Anamchara Books, 2014.

Stanley, Bruce, and Steve Hollinghurst, eds. *Earthed: Christian Perspectives on Nature Connection*. Llanguring, UK: Mystic Christ Press, 2018.

Sweeney, Theresa. *Eco-Art Therapy: Creative Activities That Let Earth Teach*. Self-published, 2013.

Thompson, Claire. *Mindfulness and the Natural World: Bringing Our Awareness Back to Nature*. London: Leaping Hare Press, 2018.

Thompson, Mary Reynolds. *Embrace Your Inner Wild: 52 Reflections for an Eco-Centric World*. Ashland, OR: White Cloud Press, 2011.

————. *Reclaiming the Wild Soul: How Earth's Landscapes Restore Us to Wholeness*. Ashland, OR: White Cloud Press, 2014.

Waddell, Helen. *Beasts and Saints*. London: Constable, 1946.

NOTES

Introduction

1. Thomas Merton, "Letter to Rosemary Radford Ruether," in *Hidden Ground of Love: Letters* (New York: Farrar, Straus, Giroux, 1985), 503.

2. David Abram, *Becoming Animal: An Earthly Cosmology* (New York: Knopf Double-day, 2010), 77–78.

3. Ada Maria Isasi-Diaz, *Mujerista Theology* (New York: Orbis Books, 1996), 125. In her book, Isasi-Diaz replaces the word *kingdom* with *kin-dom* and explains it this way: "I do not use 'kingdom' because it is obviously a sexist word that presumes God is male. Second, the concept of kingdom in our world today is both hierarchical and elitist, which is also why I do not use 'reign.' The word 'kin-dom' makes it clear that when the fullness of God becomes a day to day reality in our world, we will all be kin to each other."

4. Douglas Christie, *The Blue Sapphire of the Mind: Notes for a Contemplative Ecology* (New York: Oxford University Press, 2013), 36.

5. Pierre Teilhard de Chardin, *Divine Milieu* (New York: Harper & Row, 1960), 30.

6. Quoted in Steven Chase, *Nature as a Spiritual Practice* (Grand Rapids, MI: Wm. B. Eerdmans, 2011), 80.

7. Quoted in Phil Cousineau, *The Art of Pilgrimage* (Newburyport, MA: Conari Press, 2012), xxi.

8. You can find dried herbs at a local health-food or herbal shop. For those in the United States, Mountain Rose Organics offers very high-quality herbs that can be ordered online. In the United Kingdom, Neal's Yard Remedies sells herbs online.

9. Christine Valters Paintner, *Water, Wind, Earth, and Fire: The Christian Practice of Praying with the Elements* (Notre Dame, IN: Ave Maria Press, 2010), 9–10.

10. Charles Eisenstein, "Why the Climate Change Message Isn't Working," in *YES! Magazine* online, January 4, 2019, emphasis mine, https://www.yesmagazine.org/planet/why-the-climate-change-message-isnt-working-20190104.

1. Earth as the Original Cathedral

1. Quoted in Daniel Ladinsky, trans., *Love Poems from God: Twelve Sacred Voices from the East and the West* (New York: Penguin Books, 2002), 205.

2. See Interplay.org for more information on this exercise.

3. Colin Tudge, *The Tree: A Natural History of What Trees Are, How They Live, and Why They Matter* (New York: Three Rivers Press, 2005), xvii.

4. Abbie Farwell Brown, *The Book of Saints and Friendly Beasts* (New York: Houghton, Mifflin & Co., 1900), 83.

5. Edward Allworthy Armstrong, *Saint Francis: Nature Mystic: The Derivation and Significance of the Nature Stories in the Franciscan Legend* (Berkeley: University of California Press, 1973), 30.

6. Pierre Teilhard de Chardin, *Divine Milieu* (New York: Harper & Row, 1960), 83.

7. Peter London, *Drawing Closer to Nature: Making Art in Dialogue with the Natural World* (Boston: Shambhala, 2003), 202.

8. Mary Reynolds Thompson, *Reclaiming the Wild Soul: How Earth's Landscapes Restore Us to Wholeness* (Ashland, OR: White Cloud Press, 2014), xix.

9. John Philip Newell, *The Rebirthing of God: Christianity's Struggle for New Beginnings* (Woodstock, VT: SkyLight Paths, 2014), 3.

10. Timothy Fry, O.S.B., trans., RB 1980: *The Rule of St. Benedict* (Collegeville, MN: Liturgical Press, 1981), 58.15–16.

11. David Abram, *Becoming Animal: An Earthly Cosmology* (New York: Knopf Doubleday, 2010), 170.

12. Belden C. Lane, *Backpacking with the Saints: Wilderness Hiking as a Spiritual Practice* (New York: Oxford University Press, 2015), 211–15.

13. Jon Sweeney and Mark Burrows, *Meister Eckhart's Book of the Heart: Meditations for the Restless Soul* (Charlottesville, VA: Hampton Roads, 2017), 26.

2. Earth as the Original Scriptures

1. St. Bernard of Clairvaux, Epistola CVI, sect. 2, in *The Early English Church*, trans. Edward Churton (Whitefish, MT: Kessinger Publishing, 1840), 324.

2. Quoted in Mary C. Earle, *Celtic Christian Spirituality: Essential Writings—Annotated & Explained* (Woodstock, VT: SkyLight Paths, 2011), 75.

3. John Howard Griffin, *The Hermitage Journals: A Diary Kept While Working on the Biography of Thomas Merton* (Kansas City, MO: Andrews and McMeel, 1981), 144.

4. Quoted in Thomas Mann, *God of Dirt: Mary Oliver and the Other Book of God* (Cambridge, MA: Cowley Publications, 2004), xiii.

5. Quoted in Joseph Goldstein and Jack Kornfield, *Seeking the Heart of Wisdom: The Path of Insight Meditation* (Shambhala, 2001), 84.

6. Sharon Therese Zayac, O.P., *Earth Spirituality: In the Catholic and Dominican Tradition* (San Antonio, TX: Sor Juana Press, 2003), 43–44.

7. Sharon Blackie, *The Enchanted Life: Unlocking the Magic of the Everyday* (Tewkesbury, UK: September, 2018), 12.

8. Steven Chase, *Nature as Spiritual Practice* (Grand Rapids, MI: Wm. B. Eerdmans, 2011), 34.

9. Christine Valters Paintner, *Eyes of the Heart: Photography as a Contemplative Practice* (Notre Dame, IN: Ave Maria Press, 2013).

10. Mary Reynolds Thompson and Kate Thompson, "Inner and Outer Landscape," in *Environmental Expressive Therapies* (New York: Routledge, 2017), 78–99. I also highly recommend Mary Reynolds Thompson's book *Reclaiming the Wild Soul*.

3. Earth as the Original Saints

1. Thomas Merton, *New Seeds of Contemplation* (New York: New Directions Books, 1961), 30–31.

2. David Whyte, *River Flow: New and Selected Poems* (Many Rivers Press, 2007), 351.

3. Merton, *New Seeds of Contemplation*, 31–32.

4. Quoted in Matthew Fox, *Original Blessing: A Primer in Creation Spirituality* (New York: Jeremy Tarcher, 2000), 69.

5. This story is found on pages 93–94 of Helen Waddell's marvelous book *Beasts and Saints* (Grand Rapids, MI: Wm. B. Eerdmans, 1996), a compendium of stories of desert and Celtic monks and their encounters with animals.

6. David Steindl-Rast, O.S.B., *Gratefulness, The Heart of Prayer: An Approach to Life in Fullness* (New York: Paulist Press, 1984).

7. Barb Morris, www.BarbMorris.com, insight contributed during an online course version of this material.

8. Matsuo Basho, *The Narrow Road to the Deep North and Other Travel Sketches*, trans. Nobuyuki Yuasa (New York: Penguin, 1966), 33.

4. Earth as the Original Spiritual Directors

1. Quoted in Daniel Ladinsky, trans., *Love Poems from God: Twelve Sacred Voices from the East and the West* (New York: Penguin Books, 2002), 323.

2. Esther De Waal, *A World Made Whole: Rediscovering the Celtic Tradition* (Cleveland, OH: Fount Press, 1991), 82.

3. Thomas Merton, *The Sign of Jonas* (San Diego: Harcourt Press, 1981), 321.

4. Quoted in *Spiritual Ecology: The Cry of the Earth*, edited by Llewellyn Vaughan-Lee (Point Reyes Station, CA: The Golden Sufi Center, 2016), 23.

5. Pierre Teilhard de Chardin, *The Divine Milieu: An Essay on the Interior Life* (New York: Harper & Row, 1968), 112.

6. Helen Waddell, *Beasts and Saints* (Grand Rapids, MI: Wm. B. Eerdmans, 1996), 121.

7. Mary Oliver, "Have You Ever Tried to Enter the Long Black Branches?" in *West Wind: Poems and Prose Poems* (New York: Houghton Mifflin Company, 1997), 62.

8. St. John of the Cross, *The Collected Works of St. John of the Cross* (Washington, DC: ICS Publications, 1991).

9. Timothy Fry, O.S.B., trans., *RB 1980: The Rule of St. Benedict* (Collegeville, MN: Liturgical Press, 1981), 4:47.

5. Earth as the Original Icon

1. Quoted in Robert Van de Weyer, ed., *Celtic Fire: The Passionate Religious Vision of Ancient Britain and Ireland* (New York: Doubleday, 1990), 78.

2. Quoted in Carmen Acevedo Butcher, *A Little Daily Wisdom: Christian Women Mystics* (Brewster, MA: Paraclete Press, 2005), Kindle edition.

3. St. Bonaventure, *The Soul's Journey into God*, translated by Ewert Cousins, Classics of Western Spirituality (New York: Paulist Press, 1978), 26.

4. Walter Brueggemann, *The Prophetic Imagination* (Minneapolis, MN: Fortress Press, 2018), 117.

5. Joanna Macy, "Honoring Our Pain for the World," in *Active Hope: How to Face the Mess We're In without Going Crazy* (Novato, CA: New World Library, 2012).

6. Constance Fitzgerald, O.C.D., "Impasse and the Dark Night," in *Living with Apocalypse: Spiritual Resources for Social Compassion* (New York: HarperCollins Publishers, 1984), 94.

7. Dorothee Soelle, *Suffering* (Philadelphia: Fortress, 1975), 36.

8. St. Hildegard of Bingen, *Hildegard von Bingen's Physica: The Complete English Translation of Her Classic Work on Health and Healing* (Rochester, VT: Inner Traditions/ Bear & Company, 1998), 21.

6. Earth as the Original Sacrament

1. Quoted in Daniel Ladinsky, trans., *Love Poems from God: Twelve Sacred Voices from the East and the West* (New York: Penguin Books, 2002), 53.

2. Quoted in Andrew Linzey, *Animal Rites* (London: SCM Press, 1999), 3.

3. Quoted in Linzey, *Animal Rites*, 2.

4. Andrew Harvey, *A Journey in Ladakh: Encounters with Buddhism* (Boston: Mariner Books, 2000), 93.

5. St. Julian of Norwich, *Julian of Norwich: Showings*, translated by Edmund College and James Walsh, Classics of Western Spirituality (New York: Paulist Press, 1978), 130.

6. Gerard Manley Hopkins, "God's Grandeur," in *Gerard Manley Hopkins: Poems and Prose* (New York: Penguin Classics, 1985), 27.

7. Gerard Manley Hopkins, ibid., xx.

8. Wendell Berry, *The Selected Poems of Wendell Berry* (Berkeley, CA: Counterpoint Press, 1999), 30.

7. Earth as the Original Liturgy

1. Jon Sweeney, ed., *Phyllis Tickle: Essential Spiritual Writings* (Maryknoll, NY: Orbis Books, 2015), 1.

2. Jean-Yves Leloup, *Being Still: Reflections on an Ancient Mystical Tradition* (New York: Paulist Press, 2003), 2–8.

3. Thomas Berry, *The Great Work: Our Way into the Future* (New York: Crown, 1999), 23–24.

4. Mary C. Earle, *Celtic Christian Spirituality: Essential Writings—Annotated and Explained* (Woodstock, VT: SkyLight Paths, 2011), 33.

5. Thomas Merton, *When the Trees Say Nothing: Writings on Nature* (Notre Dame, IN: Sorin Books, 2003), 23.

6. Quoted in Jean-Yves Leloup, *Being Still: Reflections on an Ancient Mystical Tradition* (New York: Paulist Press, 2003), 83–84.

7. Thomas Merton, "Letter to Rosemary Radford Ruether," in *Hidden Ground of Love: Letters* (New York: Farrar, Straus, Giroux, 1985), 503.

8. Douglas Christie, *The Blue Sapphire of the Mind: Notes for a Contemplative Ecology* (Oxford: Oxford University Press, 2012), 317.

9. St. Bonaventure, *The Soul's Journey into God*, translated by Ewert Cousins, Classics of Western Spirituality (New York: Paulist Press, 1978), 120.

Conclusion

1. Fyodor Dostoevsky, *The Karamazov Brothers* (Hertfordshire, UK: Wordsworth Editions, 2007), 352, 356.

2. Rev. Michael J. Himes and Rev. Kenneth R. Himes, O.F.M., "The Sacrament of Creation: Toward an Environmental Theology," *Commonweal*, January 26, 1990, https://www.commonwealmagazine.org/sacrament-creation-toward-environmental-theology.

3. Thomas Berry, "The Universe Story," in *The Greening of Faith: God, the Environment, and the Good Life* (Durham, NH: University of New Hampshire Press, 2016), 215.

4. John Philip Newell, *A New Harmony: The Spirit, the Earth, and the Human Soul* (San Francisco, CA: Jossey-Bass, 2011), xiii.

5. Newell, *A New Harmony*, xiv.

6. Thomas Merton, *New Seeds of Contemplation* (New York: New Directions Books, 1961), 296.

Christine Valters Paintner is the online abbess for Abbey of the Arts, a virtual monastery offering classes and resources on contemplative practice and creative expression. She earned a doctorate in Christian spirituality from the Graduate Theological Union in Berkeley, California, and achieved professional status as a registered expressive arts consultant and educator from the International Expressive Arts Therapy Association.

Paintner is the author of thirteen books on monasticism and creativity, including *The Soul's Slow Ripening*; *Water, Wind, Earth, and Fire*; *The Artist's Rule*; *The Soul of a Pilgrim*; *Illuminating the Way*; *The Wisdom of the Body*; and a collection of poems called *Dreaming of Stones*. She leads writing retreats and pilgrimages in Ireland, Scotland, Austria, and Germany and online retreats at her website AbbeyoftheArts.com, living out her commitment as a Benedictine Oblate in Galway, Ireland, with her husband, John.

Visit Abbey of the Arts online to order a CD album of fourteen songs that companion this book and a DVD of gesture prayers to facilitate embodiment of this book's themes.

abbeyofthearts.com

Twitter: @abbeyofthearts

Facebook: @AbbeyoftheArts